Jewish Living

Reuben Turner

Illustrated by Freda Miller

VALLENTINE MITCHELL
LONDON • PORTLAND, OR

First published in 2002 in Great Britain by
VALLENTINE MITCHELL
Crown House, 47 Chase Side, Southgate
London N14 5BP

and in the United States of America by
VALLENTINE MITCHELL
c/o ISBS, 5824 N.E. Hassalo Street
Portland, Oregon 97213-3644

Website: http://www.vmbooks.com

British Library Cataloguing in Publication Data

ISBN 0-8530-3445-1 (paper)

Library of Congress Cataloguing-in-Publication Data

A catalog record for this book is available
from the Library of Congress

Typeset by Vitaset, Paddock Wood, Kent
Printed in Great Britain by Bookcraft, Midsomer Norton

To my beloved wife and life's partner
CHANNAH
and to our children and grandchildren.
May their Jewish Living bring them faith, piety and contentment.

First Edition 1982
Second Edition 1985
Third Edition 1986
Fourth Edition 2002

Also by the author
The Jewish Quiz Book. The Popular Jewish Bible Atlas
Judaism — A Way of Life (coloured filmstrip, notes/commentary)
Selections from the Seder Service (LP. record/cassette)
Living Judaism in the Jewish Youth club. Alef-Bet Word Game
Jewish Festivals. From Sabbath to Sabbath (Editor)
The Four Brothers Kusevitsky (CD)

Cover Design by Clive Bayard

PREFACE TO FOURTH EDITION

At the present time when anything to do with the meaning of the word 'tradition' is being devalued and even ignored, the standards and ethics of Jewish living, as taught by the Torah are more important than ever before. The Jewish people may be justly proud to have been the instrument that gives the clarion call to humanity in the way one should behave and conduct one's life according to God's laws and instruction. It should be remembered that other major religions have based their tenets on these principles.

I trust that this publication will continue to give encouragement to the reader of whatever age, to observe, study and understand our precious heritage, Torah Judaism.

Reuben Turner
2001

The author wishes to thank those who through their generosity have made this publication possible:-
Mr and Mrs Henry Knobil, in memory of Chaim Knobil and Isidore and Bertha Kaufmann
Alfons and Ella Silverman, in memory of Szoel and Rose Silverman and Morris and Jessie Levy
Eric and Michael Tager, in memory of their father Isser ben Meir Tager
"How great is the reward to them who perform generous acts"– *Yalkut Shimoni, Ruth*

FOREWORD
TO FIRST EDITION

It is hard to be a Jew. Any schoolchild struggling with both a secular and a religious curriculum (and the endless stream of distractions invented for him or her by the technological genius of modern man) will testify to this fact. So, too, will those housewives struggling to sustain the demanding standards of kashrut and Jewish family life against what seems an endless conspiracy to defeat their purpose. And also the business or professional man who must shred his shrinking week into ever thinner slices so as to meet the religious, communal and other demands made on his time.

It is not surprising that, in this hurried, and harried, existence, there has been an increasing tendency to observe the outer forms of Jewish religious expression and to treat as secondary the philosophy, historical experience and spiritual inspiration which underpin so much of Jewish tradition and the way of life which Judaism embraces. The danger here, of course, is that we will preserve the husk and throw away the kernel. And, while the husk itself is a vital part of the whole, it is the kernel which provides the life-giving nourishment.

There are segments of Jewry where observance in itself is almost all, where there is preserved a variety of Judaism which, for all its outward signs of strength, is a brittle thing, something to be carefully wrapped and protected against buffetings from the outside world lest it be irreparably damaged. But this is not the Judaism of most of us, who are in and of this world and who look to sustain our faith in its midst and not in some isolation ward of the devout.

It was to help stimulate and renew awareness of those basic teachings which both explain and illumine the traditional observances of the Jewish year, in the home and in the synagogue, that the JEWISH CHRONICLE turned to the Rev. Reuben Turner for advice drawn from his extensive experience as an educator. The result was a series of columns, written by him, which are both authoritative and informative. This book consists of a selection of those columns, now collected in more permanent form. If they provide not only sustenance, but also the inspiration to search even deeper into the sources of Jewish teaching, I am sure they will have achieved the author's dedicated purpose.

Geoffrey D. Paul
Editor, JEWISH CHRONICLE
1982

Contents

"JEWISH LIVING"

Introduction and Tu Bishvat

JUDAISM is made up of numerous customs and ceremonies, traditions and observances. "Jewish living" implies that they are acknowledged as an important part of the Jewish heritage and that they are experienced as a natural corollary of the Jewish way of life.

Understanding Jewish values, and making them relevant to contemporary times, greatly helps to create an appropriate atmosphere for Jewish living and for living Judaism.

The chief sources of our knowledge of Judaism are the Bible and the Talmud. It was during the talmudic period (200-511 CE) that the sages crystallised such concepts as truth, peace and justice into the general foundations of society—belief in God as Father of all; equality and brotherhood of man; humanity created for the sake of peace and friendship.

But the growth of Judaism has continued throughout the centuries. By their writings and sayings, many teachers have contributed to the great store of Jewish truth and have increased the religious and moral wealth of Judaism, always bearing in mind the axiom that "man is to live by the Law, not to die under it" (Yoma 85b).

Judaism encompasses the entire religious, cultural and social system of the Jewish people, and the heritage that has been handed down from the generation to generation has stood the test of time and truth. Its message has taught everyone — child and adult — that its laws, morals and ethics, if properly understood and practised, make for a humanity both dignified and refined.

The well-known Torah scholar, Rabbi Jonathan Eybeschuetz (1690-1764), wrote: "Judaism imposes no severe restrictions on the flesh. We are not asked to walk barefoot on snow and sleet, to wear coarse garments next to the skin, to torture the body for the good of the soul." Judaism should bring joy rather than pain; give comfort rather than cause sorrow; uplift rather than degrade.

It is fitting that this series

commences with a few words on the celebration of the New Year for Trees — Tu Bishvat. For people, like trees, need roots in order to withstand the storms and tempests of modern society. No roots can be stronger than those grown and nurtured from the seed of Jewish tradition.

During Tu Bishvat we have in mind the plants and the flowers and it is worth retelling a story related, appropriately, by Baruch Bar-Tikva, a former Soviet Prisoner of Zion now living in Israel.

It was during a trip to Czarist Russia that the Anglo-Jewish philanthropist, Sir Moses Montefiore, strongly attacked the harsh decrees against the Jews formulated by the Romanoff dynasty. Czar Alexander II welcomed the British nobleman by holding an official reception in the palace grounds.

While strolling in the gardens, the Czar told Montefiore that he had planted seventy species of flowers, representing the seventy nations of the world. Asked which flower represented the Jewish people and the land of Israel, the Czar gave no immediate reply, but merely ordered his servants to give his guest some thorns and nettles.

Montefiore replied: "Your Majesty, to my profound regret these thorns and nettles symbolise the great tragedy of my people and the land of Israel, which has been seriously neglected for 2,000 years. Yet these thorns and nettles preserve one characteristic — anyone touching them is punished."

The Talmud (Gittin 57) mentions the "joyous planting" — *netiah shel simcha* — when, on the occasion of the birth of a boy, a cedar sapling would be planted, and a cyprus sapling on the birth of a girl. In later years, it added, the wood of these trees would be used as poles for the chupa.

In modern Israel thousands of schoolchildren experience the special joy of the day by planting saplings in forests and parks throughout the country, a custom dating back to 1915, when groups of teachers in Jerusalem took their pupils to Motza to plant saplings in honour of the day. Tu Bishvat symbolises one's love for the Land and demonstrates an appreciation of trees and plants as living and fruitful creations. Going to the very roots of life, it clearly brings joy to those who observe it.

The Torah and its teachings are to the Jew what the soil is to the tree. The Shabbat and the festivals, the laws and the customs, the ceremonies and the rituals, are the very essence of "Jewish living." Just as a tree can withstand any climatic change if firmly and deeply rooted, so can a Jew survive any crisis of spirit if his faith is firm and steeped in tradition.

Marriage

THE OPENING article in this series made brief reference to the wedding canopy — the chupa — the symbolic centrepiece of the marriage ceremony. Judaism views the married state as an obligation. It is the first commandment in the Torah addressed by God to man — "Be fruitful and multiply" — and, according to Jewish teaching, it is the ideal state for the happiness of the individual and for the well-being of society at large.

Being divinely instituted, it is naturally invested with a highly sacred character, showing equality to man and woman alike. The Bible narrative, indeed, records as much about the Matriarchs, Sarah, Rebecca, Leah and Rachel, as it does about the Patriarchs, Abraham, Isaac and Jacob.

The last section of the Proverbs, recited every Sabbath eve by the husband, pays the finest tribute to womanly virtue and woman's worth. The Talmud, too, includes numerous references extolling married life and placing great emphasis on the high esteem in which the wife is held.

As in so much of Jewish living, it is the Bible, in the story of the first recorded marriage — that of Rebeccah and Isaac — which demonstrates the procedure for those ready to take the most important step in their lives.

The sidra of Chaye Sarah (Genesis 24) suggest the importance of choosing one's partner from among one's own people: a young man has to ask the girl of his choice for her consent before seeking the approval of her parents and the young couple should look for signs of a good character in each other, including thoughtfulness, kindness and modesty.

The sources say that it is the man's responsibility to search for and choose his life's partner since, as the Talmud states, "... the mitzva devolves on the part of the man, for one who has lost a treasure must go and seek it for himself; the treasure does not go looking for him" (Kiddushin 20a), referring to the fact that Adam lost his rib in the creation of Eve.

The Talmud adds: "Love thy wife as thyself and honour her more than thyself. Be careful not to cause woman to weep, for God counts her tears. Israel was redeemed from Egypt on account of the virtue of its women. He who weds a good woman is as if he had fulfilled all the precepts of the Torah."

The custom of the *aufruff*, or "calling up," of the groom on the Shabbat before his wedding dates back to Temple times, when bridegrooms passed through a special gate and were greeted by well-wishers with congratulations and blessings. This custom has continued in the synagogue and the old practice of showering the bridegroom with nuts and raisins after his "call-up" is being revived.

The marriage ceremony itself, and the sacred character in which it is held, is indicated by the Hebrew word *kiddushin*, "sanctification." It is regarded as being part of the scheme of Creation and provides for man's happiness and completeness.

Of note is the fact that the numerical value (*gematria*) of the Hebrew word for "love," *ahava*, equals that of the Hebrew word for "one," *echad*. The marriage is designed to unite a couple in love in an ever-sacred partnership.

The nine Hebrew words commencing with *"harei at mekudeshet,"* said by the groom on placing the ring on the bride's forefinger, form a dignified resolution to lead a joint life according to the teachings and traditions of Judaism.

The seven blessings, *sheva berachot,* recited under the chupa, identify the young couple with the story of Creation, the history of Israel and its future hopes and aspirations.

The wedding ceremony opens and closes with the blessing over wine, symbolic of the joyousness that is the hallmark of the marriage service. Bride and groom drink from both cups of wine, an indication of their resolve to share in everything they do during their life together.

In the world to come, says the Talmud (Shabbat 31a), the first three questions to be asked of man when being judged on his earthly life are, "Did you buy and sell in good faith? Did you have time for study? Did you raise a family?" In other words, the three important attributes a person is deemed to require are sincere dealings with others, educational improvement and marriage.

"Jewish living" implies upholding the pillars on which humanity supports itself and the chupa is one of the main pillars on which the future of Jewry depends.

Consecration of a Home

SINCE THE Jewish home is considered a "miniature sanctuary" — *mikdash m'at* — it is appropriate that it should be modelled on the lines of the Temple. The Book of Numbers tells of the first dedication ceremony for any kind of building, when the tabernacle and its contents were sanctified by Moses.

On the completion of the Temple, King Solomon arranged an elaborate service of consecration vividly described in the First Book of Kings. At a later stage in history, the Maccabees rededicated the Temple after its despoliation by the Greeks.

The significance of the ceremony is of great importance to those setting up a new home, since Judaism assigns to the home centrality in its theme of holiness. The life which the Jew is expected to follow has its roots in the home: it is the training-ground for the moulding of character, habits, action, speech and thought.

In the home the ideals of charity, hospitality, kindliness and other virtues are taught and exemplified. Nor is it to be an isolated area wherein a family lives withdrawn from society; rather a place radiating the teachings of Judaism outside its walls through the example set by those within them.

By maintaining a warm Jewish home, one's association with Judaism and its purpose is both positive and strong. It results in contentment for those living in it, and in the creation of a centre of love and co-operation.

All these attributes are high expectations, and human beings, limited as they are, can only aspire to perfection. To start out on the road towards fulfilling these aspirations a get-together is called which is not only in the nature of a housewarming, but which is elevated into a significant, if brief, religious ceremony.

As a symbol of prosperity and as a reminder of the Temple and the altar, bread and salt are among the first things brought into a new home. Later the first "official" act — the dedication of the house, *chanucat habayit* — takes place.

The ceremony opens with the fixing of the mezuzah on the upper part of the right doorpost of each room in a slanting position, accompanied by the recitation of appropriate blessings and suitable verses from Psalm 119 which make up the Hebrew word *berachah*, "blessing."

This psalm, which starts with the declaration "With my whole heart have I sought thee . . .," is regarded as

being particularly appropriate for the consecration of a Jewish home because, say the rabbis, one of the foundations on which the Jewish home rests is loving obedience to God.

In the belief that the Divine Providence permeates the life of all mankind, and to implant this principle in our minds, the Torah commands one to affix a mezuzah to the entrance of every home and on the doorpost of every room, a permanent visual-aid to be seen day and night.

Both on the reverse of the parchment and on the case itself, the Hebrew word *Shadai* (Almighty) is inscribed. One interpretation given is that the letters are an abbreviation for *shomer daltot Yisrael* — the Almighty is the guardian over the doors of Israel.

The words of the mezuzah (taken from Deuteronomy 6:4-9 and 11:13-21) are to be written on 22 lines, corresponding to the number of letters in the Hebrew alphabet. The last sentence is: "That your days may be multiplied, and the days of your children, in the land which the Lord swore unto your fathers to give them, as the days of heaven upon the earth."

The concluding words, *al ha'aretz* ("upon the earth"), must form a line on their own. The seventeenth-century talmudist, the Taz, explains that the words "heaven" and "earth" should be separated from each other as far as possible. By setting out the sentence in this manner, the phrases "that your days may be multiplied" and "the days of your children" equal in magnitude the distance between heaven and earth.

Hospitality

HAVING MADE their home a "miniature sanctuary," the newly married couple become "priest" and "priestess" in their new abode, a place wherein peace and harmony should reign supreme. In fact, on entering that other sanctuary — the synagogue — one proclaims the words used by the non-Jewish prophet, Balaam, on seeing the Children of Israel living in the desert in harmony and contentment: *"Mah tovu ohalecha Ya'acov,* How goodly are your homes, O Jacob, your dwelling places, O Israel" (Numbers 24).

The Talmud lays great stress on *shalom bayit,* domestic harmony. It states in tractate Derech Eretz 2: "He who loves his wife as much as himself honours her more than himself; he who rears his children in the right manner, that man will have peace in his household."

The seventeenth-century Isaac ben Eliakim, of Posen, wrote an ethical work, "Lev Tov" (A Good Heart) and, in the chapter on marriage, enumerated "Ten commandments for a wife." The tenth states: "Be careful to guard against jealousy. Do not say anything that might hurt him (your husband). If you treat him like a king, then he, in turn, will treat you like a queen."

Our sages warn against dissension among couples: "A home where there is dissension will not last" (Derech Eretz Zuta 9). In "Avot d'Rabbi Natan" 28, Rabbi Shimon ben Gamliel cautions: " . . . he who brings jealously and strife into his house is as if he brought them among all Israel." The home has to be a virtual *ir miklat,* "city of refuge," from a hostile world.

"Hospitality is even more important and meritorious than greeting the glory of the Divine Presence" (Shabbat 127a). Love of God leads to love of man; the Talmud cites the example of Abraham, who broke off a conversation with God to welcome the three travellers he had sighted in the distance.

Abraham taught the world the virtues of kindness and charity by having a home with four entrances, one in each direction, so that the

wayfarer could enter the house by the quickest possible route and leave by a different exit in order not to be embarrassed by those passing (Midrash Tehillim 110).

The same source points out that the words "and he planted" are mentioned only twice in the Torah, when God planted a garden in Eden (Genesis 2:8) and when Abraham planted a fruit-tree in Beersheba (Genesis 21:33), suggesting that anyone who practises the mitzva of hospitality will merit Paradise (Gan Eden) in the world to come.

The inhabitants of Jerusalem during Temple times were renowned for their acts of hospitality, especially during the *shalosh regalim* (three pilgrim festivals), when Jews from throughout the Holy Land would converge on Jerusalem. Even during the rest of the year, the Talmud relates, " . . . in Jerusalem it was customary to display a flag at the door to indicate that the meal was ready and anyone might enter and eat" (Baba Batra 93b).

In biblical times and throughout the

Middle Ages it was the duty and responsibility of the communal leaders to provide food and shelter for travellers and visitors. Most synagogues had special lodging houses for this purpose and the kiddush made in the synagogue on Sabbath eve is reminiscent to this day of those occasions when the chazan would recite kiddush for the benefit of the visitors.

In some communities special hospitality *(hachnasat orchim)* societies were maintained to help visitors find comfort and kindness in strange surroundings. The opportunity of giving hospitality occurs daily, but more so on Shabbat and the festivals, and it is considered a particular duty to have guests on Purim, at the seder and in the succah.

The term *hachnasat orchim* is not restricted merely to the provision of food and shelter, but includes an open house for meetings to discuss communal needs and for the giving of charity. And Judaism urges that acts of kindness be accompanied by smiles.

Says Shammai in tractate Avot: "Greet all persons cordially. If a man gives his fellow even the richest gift in the world, but with a grim face, the Torah considers that gift to be nothing. But he who greets his fellow human being in a friendly manner, even if he has nothing to give, is considered to have given the finest gift of all."

On the other hand, the thirteenth-century "Sefer Chasidim" states: "The guest should not be watched too attentively at the table, as it may embarrass him and he will refrain from eating fully."

The story is told of the Chasidic rebbe who had guests at his table every Shabbat and who, immediately after kiddush, would intentionally upset some wine on the tablecloth in order not to discomfort any guest who might spill wine or food during the meal.

The virtue of compassion encompasses not only consideration towards humans, but also the treatment of animals and birds; if they are domesticated, they must be fed before one sits down to eat (Berachot 40a).

Charity

ACCORDING TO Maimonides (Yad, Matnot Aniyim 10; 7), the highest of the eight rungs in the degrees of charity is when one helps a man to help himself; to assist him to rehabilitate himself from his present state of having to accept charity.

The Hebrew word for charity, *tzedakah,* denotes far more than helping the under-privileged and the poor. It implies "justice," "piety," "righteousness" in everything one says or does. The word is first mentioned in the Bible as a characteristic of Abraham (Genesis 15:6 and 18:19): "For I have known him, that he may instruct his children and his posterity . . . to do righteousness (*tzedakah*) and justice."

Love rather than pity has always influenced Jewish benevolence, which in reality is only one aspect of the wider term for kindly acts, *gemilut chasadim,* according to the Mishna "one of the three pillars on which the world is based" (Avot, 1).

The rabbis were quick to point out, however, that even in the giving of charity one must be sensible; they estimated one-tenth of one's income as being a fair allocation for this purpose, giving one-fifth as the ceiling.

The maxim "charity begins at home" may well have originated from this ruling, since earned income was to be spent not only on providing the normal requirements of a Jewish home, such as food and clothing, but on the means by which a good education could be received,

maintained and improved.

Maimonides ruled that before donating to a communal fund, one should make sure that its administration was honest, prudent and efficient. However, when giving money to the poor, it was praiseworthy to give anonymously and without pomp, sparing any embarrassment to the recipient.

The Talmud has much to say on the giving of charity and its importance in the Jewish way of life. On the subject of longevity, it relates that Rabbi Nechuniah's disciples asked him: "What have you done to prolong your life?" He answered: "I have been generous with my money" (Megillah 28).

The obligation to give away part of one's possessions falls on every Jew, and even "the poor man who is himself maintained by charity should give charity" (Gittin 6), for in Judaism all possessions are regarded as belonging to God and each and every person is merely a guardian of God's wealth.

In the Jewish home, charitable acts become second nature. The housewife, before kindling the Sabbath or festival lights, will drop some coins into the charity box. Before Yom Kippur, distribution of money will be made to numerous charitable appeals — since "repentance, prayer and charity avert the evil decree," according to the familiar "Unesaneh Tokef" prayer.

Fancy-dress groups call on Jewish homes on Purim to collect money for specific charities; house-to-house drives are made for Israeli and refugee appeals in order to alleviate social distress. Throughout the year there are opportunities for fulfilling the mitzva of charity.

There is, in fact, no way in which one can disregard this biblical obligation, since *tzedakah* is both a positive and a negative command, following each other in Deuteronomy 15.

Chassidic folklore is replete with tales of charitable giving. The wife of a famous rebbe remarked to him: "Your prayer was so long today. Do you think that, through your efforts, the wealthy will be more generous in

their gifts to the poor?" The rebbe replied: "At least half of my prayer has been accomplished. The poor are willing to accept the gifts."

The need for an immediate response to charitable requests is illustrated by the story of the congregant who asked his rabbi why it was not necessary to make a blessing when giving charity, as was done when performing other mitzvot.

The rabbi told him: "If a blessing were required for this mitzva, then one might make the excuse that one is not clean enough to pronounce a prayer and one would have to wash one's hands first. So, in order not to delay the act of charity, the Torah has not demanded the saying of a blessing."

Prompt action can save from ruin a person or family worthy of sympathy and in need of encouragement. As Solomon warned: "Withhold not good from them to whom it is due when it is in the power of your hand to do it" (Proverbs 3).

If parents are in need of help, children are obliged to carry out the commandment of *tzedakah,* for the poor of one's own household take precedence over the poor of one's city. Moreover, the poor inhabitants of Eretz Yisrael take precedence over the poor inhabitants of the diaspora (Yoreh Deah 251).

Neighbours and Friends

JUDAISM STRESSES the need for constant improvement in the realm of human relations. It was the talmudical Ben Azai who declared that the foundation of the Jewish religion was to be found in Genesis 5:1: "This is the book of the generations of Adam. In the day that God created man, he made him in the likeness of God."

Translating the Hebrew word *adam* in this context as "man," Ben Azai interprets its use to suggest that all mankind can trace its origins to one parent and all human beings are therefore brothers. This, he says, is the concept of humanity and of the brotherhood of man.

Moreover, since each individual is created in the divine image, each must be treated with respect and honour, in the same way as one is expected to show reverence towards the Creator.

The prophet Malachi spoke on a similar theme: "Have we not all one father?" he asked. "Has not one God created us?"

A couple setting up a new home will soon have dealings with their associates and neighbours in a wide range of activities which require a warm relationship if they are to continue living in harmony with one another.

In Jewish living various considerations and conditions, outlined below, have to be taken into account which bring out the characteristic known as *ahavat haberiyot*, the regard and dignity to which a person is entitled. This concept equates with *ahavat Hashem*, the love and esteem for the Almighty, the combination of the two making for perfect human relationships.

In the normal course of events, people can either attract or offend those with whom they come into contact by their actions and speech. Judaism demands that our behaviour creates a *kiddush Hashem*, sanctification of God's name, and such emotions as jealousy, deception and revenge run counter to its teachings. The rabbis say that to behave otherwise is to risk the evils of slander, gossip and hatred.

Tolerance, understanding and sympathy are more easily created by meeting one's friends and neighbours with a happy disposition. As the rabbis have stated: "... Welcome everyone with a cheerful countenance" (Avot 1).

Our sages stress that *all* humanity must be treated with honour and respect, regardless of whether or not they are of one's type or hail from a similar background.

A Chasidic story illustrates this point. The famous Gerrer Rebbe had heard that some of his followers had developed a custom of helping only those who were among their associates; strangers were excluded.

During the sermon the Rebbe remarked that among the list of birds proscribed by the Torah was the stork (Leviticus 11). Its Hebrew name, *chassidah,* stemmed from the word for kindness and benevolence since, the Talmud explained (Chullin 63), the stork had the habit of bringing food to the nests of its own kind.

If this were the case, said the Rebbe, and it was such a helpful bird, why were we not permitted to eat it? Because, he replied, it fed only its own kind, and not outsiders.

The making of friends is regarded as a true achievement, particularly with regard to one who had previously been hostile. "He is a strong man who can turn his enemy into a friend" (Avot d'Rabbi Natan 23).

The famous Gaon of Vilna, in a letter of advice to his family, wrote: "Treat all men with respect and amiability. Bring happiness to each other by kindly social relations. Let there be no dissension of any kind, but let love and brotherliness reign. Forgive one another and live in amity for the sake of God."

The Torah commands us to love our friends and neighbours to such an extent that if we see them doing wrong, we should, with tact and discretion, convince them of their mistake. This is, however, to be done privately and gently so as not to cause them embarrassment.

But such advice may be given only when there is a likelihood of the offender taking notice, for, as it is stated in Proverbs, "do not reprove an arrogant man, or he will hate you; reprove a wise man, and he will love you."

Maimonides states that the commandment in Leviticus 19 — "You shall not hate your brother in the heart" — suggests that one must not bear a silent hatred (in one's heart), but rather discuss the cause of the matter frankly and be prepared to forgive any misunderstandings.

Nor should one say anything insulting or humiliating, since this is likely to cause unpleasantness (Yad Deot 6). We are required to "judge every person charitably," *dan l'chaf zechut*, to find some kind of meritorious motivation in the sayings and actions of others.

Meal time

HAVING BEEN sent out of the Ark by Noah to find an olive, the dove said to God: "Sovereign of the Universe! Let my food be as bitter as the olive but from *your* hand, rather than as sweet as honey and from the hand of a human being" (Sanhedrin 108).

The Talmud tells this story to illustrate that people prefer to be self-sufficient in their own home and at their own table, rather than having to rely on others for food, however tasty the latter's menu may be. As we say in grace after meals, "Let me not be in the need of the gifts of human hands, or of their loans."

Whether one eats at home or with family or friends, mealtime in Judaism takes on a special significance. Any meal which involves the eating of man's "staple food," bread (even an amount no bigger than an olive), qualifies for a number of interesting rituals.

In Judaism the benefits of life, so often either ignored or taken for granted, are made to be remembered as products of God's continual goodness. Even so routine an act as eating is elevated to a higher plane and made into an act of consecration.

The meal has blessings both before and after it and connected with each of the blessings are a number of customs which give the meal an added dimension. Thus, eating is more than just another function which one performs in order to stay alive.

Before the start of a meal, one ensures that, just as one has laid out the cutlery, one has instinctively placed salt as an essential item on the table. The table in the Jewish home represents the altar of Temple times,

and "... with all your offerings you shall offer salt." The entire presentation of the table should be in keeping with a sanctified act and a sacred place.

The salt, moreover, reminds us of the wondrous ways of the Almighty. The rabbis of the Talmud regarded the fact that, after being dissolved, it can again become crystallised as an example of God's gifts which remind us that food is Heaven-sent and not man-made.

Salt is manufactured through two opposing forces — fire and water — both producing the food of the earth. The fire of the sun ripens the crops; the water irrigates the fields, emphasising the psalmists words, "How great are thy works, O Lord; thy thoughts are very deep" (Psalm 92, 6).

Preceding the meal itself, the ritual of *netilat yadayim* (washing of the hands) takes place, in the same way as the priests washed their hands before they performed their sacred duties in the Temple (Aruch Hashulchan 159). This is followed by the blessing over the bread, *ha'motzi*, and the sprinkling of the salt on bread.

All ten fingers are placed on the bread while the blessing is said, as ten mitzvot are involved from the time the seed is planted until it becomes bread (Tur Orach Chayim 167). The blessing itself contains ten words.

The Talmud (Berachot 3) states that "he who prolongs his meal prolongs his life." And Rabbi Nachman of Bratslav (1772-1810) advised, "A man should eat slowly and with etiquette *even if alone at the table*."

At the end of the meal, *birkat hamazon*, grace after meals, is recited, according to instruction in the Torah, "And you shall eat and be satisfied and bless the Lord your God for the good land which He has given you" (Deuteronomy 8). The rabbis ruled that the words should be understood by the person reciting them.

Immediately before grace, all remaining knives are removed from the table. This custom stems from the latter-day role of the Jewish home in place of the Temple, and of the table in place of the altar. No instrument of steel or iron was allowed to be used in the building of the Temple or to be placed on the altar.

It is said that on one occasion a person reciting grace became so emotional while referring to the rebuilding of Jerusalem that he stabbed himself with a knife lying on the table (Orach Chayim 180).

There is another custom to leave bread on the table during grace. The sages suggest that although we may have completed our meal, there may yet be a knock on the door from a poor person or visitor requiring a meal, and the bread remains on the table in readiness for such an eventuality.

An unusual "Amen" is inserted in the middle of grace. Customarily, this is said in response to a blessing made by someone else, but during grace it is added after the blessing for the rebuilding of Jerusalem. This is because, following that blessing, the biblical section of grace is concluded and that which follows was instituted by the rabbis.

וְאָכַלְתָּ וְשָׂבַעְתָּ וּבֵרַכְתָּ

Dietary Laws

THE PREVIOUS article made the point that even through the routine act of eating, one can serve God and not merely satisfy one's appetite. At the same time, we identify ourselves with *knesset Yisrael,* the brotherhood of Israel, by reciting the same blessings and grace and observing the same rituals which are an integral part of the meal.

By the observance of kashrut, the dietary laws, the Jew expresses his links with time-hallowed Judaism and with communal responsibilities. These laws, together with the other mitzvot, constitute the foundations upon which the Jewish people have survived and whose purpose is to make the Jews "a kingdom of priests and a holy nation" (Exodus 19).

The Torah, which gives the Jew his prescription for healthy living, sets out the laws which create self-sanctification through positive means. Commenting on the verse in Deuteronomy 14, "For you are a people consecrated to the Eternal your God," the rabbis remark: sanctify yourself with the things that are permitted to you (Sifri).

A well-known tag asserts that "a person is what he eats"; the character of a person will, in time, assume the qualities of the food and drink he consumes. Scientists have demonstrated how the food one eats has a particular effect on the body and in consequence, the mind.

This is the purpose of the laws of kashrut and the restricted diet it imposes on the Jew. In order to obtain a positive spiritual attitude towards life, the law disciplines one towards holiness through exercising control over all food.

The thirteenth-century Cabalist, Azriel ben Solomon, stated that "... all the dietary laws mentioned in the Torah have the words, 'Be holy unto Me,' added to the text, in order to purify the soul, which draws its sustenance from the food in accordance with its refinement and purity."

Physiologists accept that food in general affects not only the physical health of man, but his entire mental outlook. Body and soul are nowhere so closely connected as through diet.

Kashrut is also conducive to self-restraint, a forceful discipline in the formation of character and conduct. Ben Zoma asks: "Who is strong? He who subdues his desires (Avot 4)."

The dietary laws do not just impose restrictions; they teach moral freedom.

They belong to the category of mitzvot known as *chukim,* laws whose reason cannot be known with any apparent certainty. Maimonides tried to find a logical reason for all the commandments — and advanced health and hygiene for the kashrut laws — but maintained in two of his major works that "... we must not allow our inability to find the ultimate reason for these laws to influence our obedience to them."

Recent medical research has established that certain animals are both disease-spreading and disease-inducing. It is these very animals that are non-kosher.

Those birds which seize their prey in a cruel manner are forbidden. And Nachmanides suggests that fish which have no fins and scales — the proscribed variety — usually live in the lower levels of the water and lack the warmth of the sun, making them less wholesome than those living in the clear, upper reaches.

The biblical commentator, Ibn Ezra, states that flesh that is eaten becomes part of the body of the one who eats it; while the mediaeval teacher, Menachem Rekanati, put it this way: "For the human soul it is of the greatest importance whether the body consists of fine or coarse material. Even the lights shine brighter through a good lamp and some trees yield different fruit according to the soil in which they are planted."

Everything in the kitchen and on the table is governed by the dietary laws. The most visible feature is a double set of kitchen utensils, towels, crockery and cutlery, one each for meat and milk dishes.

Kosher meat is under strict supervision from the moment the animal is slaughtered to the time the food reaches the table. Only a man of learning and piety, a shochet, may kill an animal by means of shechita, the Jewish ritual method, which causes immediate unconsciousness and no unnecessary suffering.

The animal or fowl is then inspected to ascertain that it is not diseased or otherwise flawed. From the wholesaler it passes to a butcher licensed by the kashrut authorities to sell kosher meat.

Before it is cooked, the meat must be totally drained of blood, as commanded in Leviticus 7, "You must not consume any blood, either of fowl or of animal." This is done either by soaking and salting or by broiling over a flame.

Other aspects of kashrut (which will be detailed in subsequent articles) include the purchase of approved wines; the checking of vegetables, fruit and nuts to make sure they are free of insects; knowing the ingredients of bread, cakes, cereals and confectionery; and checking the oil used in tinned foods (such as fish).

After eating meat one should wait three hours (some wait six) before eating or drinking any dairy product; after drinking milk or eating cheese, thirty minutes must pass before one may consume meat.

The observance of kashrut commences at an even earlier stage than the purchase of food and drink, cooking and serving. Any utensils used for eating, for the preparation of food or for storing food require immersion in a special mikva (pool of pure water) which is often situated near the synagogue. This practice is known as *tevilat keilim.*

Family Purity

AMONG archaeological discoveries in Israel since the establishment of the State was the mountain fortress of Massada. Here were uncovered the records, over eighteen hundred years old, of those who gave their lives for the holy soil of Eretz Yisrael.

Of all the discoveries made, perhaps the most fascinating were the two mikvaot, which experts confirm were built according to the minutest requirements of Jewish law.

A recent visitor to Russia reported that he was taken to a building where, under a pile of boxes, a false floor and floorboards, was a staircase leading to a small pool. "This is the city's mikvaot, which experts confirm were used regularly by our forty families."

Listening to the details of how the mikvah had been built under unbelievable circumstances, the visitor asked why, with all the expense and danger involved, the local community had taken the trouble. "Without it," came the reply, "we could not live as Jews."

With the separation of eighteen hundred years between the events of Massada and those of Russia, neither the mikvah nor its significance to Jewish life has diminished in stature. The purpose and the spiritual link between the generations remains identical and intact.

Many modern Jews would be surprised to learn that the mikvah is of greater importance than the synagogue or the Scroll of the Law. Jewish law rules that a congregation which does not possess its own mikvah does not have the status of a "community" (Orech Chayim 468). Synagogue services may be held in a house, a hall or even a shop, but a mikvah has to be *mayim chaim*, a fountain of living water, and this can only be achieved in a purpose-built structure. A *sefer Torah*, in fact, may be sold to provide funds for the building of a mikvah.

The Hebrew word "mikvah" means a "ritual pool of water," originating from the term *mikvei mayim* (Genesis 1:10) in the story of the Creation, but it may also be interpreted to mean "hope." In the Talmud (Yoma 85b) Rabbi Akiva conveys the teaching that the two meanings are one.

Quoting the Prophet's use of *mikvei Yisrael*, the "hope of Israel" (Jeremiah 17:13), Rabbi Akiva asserts that the people's future is protected and guaranteed by the observance of the mikvah laws, which are a corner-stone for the survival of Israel.

Jewish and non-Jewish authorities alike have affirmed that the laws of family purity *(taharat ha'mishpachah)* are the key to marital happiness, bringing with it mutual understanding, consideration and respect. The laws enable husband and wife to have a life-long courtship, bringing to their marriage a constant freshness which enhances the most important relationship in a person's life. The couple are united in an ever-sacred partnership blessed by God.

The Hebrew letter *mem* has many connotations. The Midrash (Bereshit Rabbah 81) explains Jeremiah's declaration "The Lord, God, is Truth — *Emet*" (Jeremiah 10:10), by stating that God's seal is Truth, the Hebrew spelling of which, *emet*, is aleph, mem and tav.

These letters are the first, middle and last letters of the alphabet. In other words, God says, "I am first, and I am last" (Isaiah 44), with the letter mem representing transition and change.

This is illustrated in another way by the word *emet*. The first two letters spell out the word *em*, "mother" — the beginning of man — and the last two letters form the word *met*, "death" — the end of man. Again, the middle letter, mem, of *emet* implies the present, the transitory state between past and future.

In the same way, say the rabbis, the letter mem stands for mikvah, breaking down the barriers of time and taking us outside its limitations, thereby making us more God-like and placing in Him our hope for the future.

The benefits of the laws of family purity are threefold: they contribute to renewed and mutual love, they exert control over one's passions, and they provide an aid to healthy living, physically and spiritually. These results have been verified — if, indeed, such verification were needed — throughout the world of science and medicine.

The bride's prayer, customarily recited before her first immersion in the mikvah, was composed by Rabbi Raphael Meldola (1754-1828). It expresses the hope and anticipation of the "wonderful adventure of building a sanctified home in Israel on sound foundations and on the truth of the Torah laws.

"... a marriage in which there will never come between my husband and me any anger or bitterness, any jealousy or envy, but in which there will be between us only love and fraternity, peace and comradeship, humility, meekness and patience; in which there will be love, charity and kindliness and the doing of good deeds to all creatures."

Children

THROUGHOUT the ages, the birth of a child in a Jewish home has been greeted not only with profound joy, but with a sense of hope for the future and for the survival of the Jewish people in a hostile world.

Within a few hours of its birth, a baby girl receives her Hebrew name after her father has been called up to the Torah. In the case of a boy, the naming awaits his brit milah (circumcision) on the eighth day after his birth.*

In Temple times a new mother was obliged to offer a special sacrifice; today she goes to synagogue, as soon as possible after the confinement, both to hear the Reading of the Law and to express thanksgiving and gratitude for the precious gift bestowed upon her by God.

The naming of a child is not to be taken lightly. The Talmud relates that Rabbi Meir could establish the character of a person by analysing his name. And in his book, "Michtav M'Eliyahu," the late Rabbi Eliyahu Dessler states that people are called by names which reveal their character to others, even to the extent of alerting them to their faults.

The role and responsibilities of both father and mother towards the child are soon apparent. The parent is the child's principal teacher — and not only in the early years. The words added during the grace after meals, *avi mori* (my father, my teacher) and *imi morati* (my mother, my teacher), are a constant reminder of this important parental function.

The Hebrew words *horim* and *morim*, parents and teachers, not only sound the same, but have similar meanings — to teach, to instruct. In the first confessional passage of the Yom Kippur "Al Chet," the two words are in fact classified together.

In the first paragraph of the Shema, the Torah instructs: "And you shall teach them diligently to your children and speak of them when you sit in your home ..." (Deuteronomy 6:7). From the word "speak" the rabbis

The practical aspects of brit milah and pidyon haben (redemption of the first-born) will be dealt with in a subsequent article.

deduce: "When a child begins to speak, the father should speak the sacred tongue with him and teach him Torah."

The teaching of living Judaism should begin as soon as the child becomes aware of its surroundings. Learning easy Hebrew passages, listening to Jewish stories, playing records and cassettes with Hebrew songs, using Hebrew letter-blocks and similar toys, looking at picture-books depicting religious themes — all these add to the child's Jewish identity and sense of awareness.

It takes no time at all before he or she begins to appreciate the Jewish heritage and culture which will be studied — and enjoyed — in later years. The child equipped with this kind of background will have a head start once it joins kindergarten or school: the tuition given there will supplement the training received at home.

A favourite custom to induce children to learn the aleph bet was to take biscuits covered with honey and

cut out shapes of the various letters which the child had to learn. As soon as the letter could be identified and named, the child was allowed to eat it.

A sound parent-child relationship is cemented through the ceremony of "blessing the children" done by the father or mother, or both, on Shabbat and festival evenings before the recitation of Kiddush. The son receives the blessing given by Jacob to Joseph's sons: "May God make you like Ephraim and Menasseh"; the daughter's blessing is associated with the good deeds and virtues of the Matriarchs: "May God make you like Sarah, Rebecca, Rachel and Leah." This meaningful ritual does much to foster respect towards parents and to encourage the child to regard them as spiritual advisors.

Parents are, of course, only too aware of the problems involved in raising children. In fact, the term *tza'ar giddul banim*, "the pain of raising children," originates with Jacob, whom the Talmud cites as being the classic example of a father who suffered untold grief through the actions of his children.

But parents accept the difficulties as a natural part of their child's development towards adolescence and maturity, receiving as compensation for their patience and energy the moments of nachas which come from time to time. The reward for devoting utmost strength to the adequate upbringing of children is first mentioned in relation to Abraham, whom God praised for this action more than for any other.

The Bible also gives advice regarding punishment for any wrongdoing in children. "He who spares the rod hates his child" (Proverbs 13), and "Withhold not from punishing a child: if you will apply the rod, he will not die from it" (Proverbs 23).

A talmudic passage stresses the importance attached to parental example — "What the child speaks out of doors he has learned indoors" (Succah 56) — and on favouritism it declares: "One should not favour one child above the others" (Shabbat 10).

Redemption of the First Born

IMMEDIATELY after the last of the Ten Plagues — the slaying of the Egyptian first-born males — God sanctified the first-born of Israel and designated to them the sacred service in the Tabernacle (Exodus 13).

This commandment of sanctity also applied to the first-born of the flock and the first fruits of the trees, which were brought as sacrifices to the Temple (Numbers 8). However, after the incident of the Golden Calf, in which the first-born also participated, the *b'chorim* (first born) were deemed to be unfit to serve God and their place was taken by the tribe of Levi, who had not taken part in worshipping the calf (Bemidbar Rabbah 4).

The Torah gives details of the replacement (Numbers 18) and the necessity for "redemption," called *pidyon b'chor* (redemption of the first-born), which later became popularly known as *pidyon haben* (redemption of the son), listing those who qualify for the mitzva.

The child must be the mother's first; the ceremony must take place on the thirty-first day after the birth (but if this date coincides with Shabbat or Yomtov, then immediately afterwards); and the amount for the redemption is to equal five shekels of (pure) silver (96 gramme), to be given to the Cohen, a member of the priestly family of Aaron.

Judaism teaches that the first and best of everything, together with the first-born of every creature, belongs to God: they have a special value in His order of the universe. Throughout the Bible, the word "first" has a significance and sanctity which those following do not possess.

On the occasion of the birth of a first-born son, when the parents are filled with joy and thanksgiving, the short ceremony of *pidyon haben* leaves an indelible imprint in their minds of the influence Divine Providence has on their lives. In Jewish living, there are many similar reminders that fulfilment and purpose in life are to be found in one's acceptance and understanding of the mitzvot.

The obligation to redeem the son is on the father. If, for some reason, the boy has not been redeemed by the age

of barmitzvah, it is the father's duty to attend to the redemption ceremony then, or when the son reaches a more mature age (Aruch Ha'Shulchan 225). The Talmud states quite clearly that if the father fails to redeem him, the son has to redeem himself when he grows up (Kiddushin 29b).

It was during the Gaonic period (600-1050) that the ritual for the ceremony as we know it today was formulated; the Torah itself does not spell out the formula for the redemption.

Those attending the pidyon haben begin by sitting down to a festive meal *(seudat mitzva)*. After the grace before meals, the proceedings are interrupted by the father carrying in the child on an ornate tray, which is usually adorned by jewellery and other attractive objects. The father places the tray on the table and, at the same time, holds the five coins.

The ceremony consists of a dialogue between the Cohen and the father. "Which do you prefer? To give me your first-born or to redeem him for five coins?" asks the Cohen. "I prefer to redeem my son," the father replies. "Here is his redemption money, as I am obliged to give according to the commandment of the Torah."

Several biblical quotations, the priestly blessing and, as usual on any joyous occasion, the blessing over wine conclude this brief but impressive ceremony.

The core of the ceremony is in the handing of the money to the Cohen. The Talmud rules (Berachot 51a) that

if the money were lost before it was handed over, the redemption would be considered as not having taken place.

After the ceremony the Cohen normally gives the money to charity. The Midrash (Bereshit Rabbah, Vayeishev 84) explains the five shekels of silver as being the sum for which Joseph was sold by his brothers.

The precise date of the ceremony is considered so important that if parent and child are not in the same place on the thirty-first day, the father may arrange to redeem the child from a Cohen wherever he is, with a slight modification of the formula normally used when both are present.

Short and simple is this impressive ceremony which frees the first-born from his priestly vocation and places him among the family to carry out the holy calling of being a Jew in the home. The outstanding halachic authority and Sephardi rabbi, the Rivash (1326-1407), wrote that the first-born has the same special obligation to influence family life that would have been his had he carried out the sacred service in the sanctuary: the sanctity of an individual cannot be nullified.

Not every first-born is subject to the redemption ceremony. Those who are exempt include the child of a Cohen or Levite, or of the daughter of a Cohen or Levite; a child following a miscarriage (after the third month of pregnancy); and a child delivered by Caesarean section.

In 1974 the Bank of Israel began striking special "redemption" coins which have the exact silver content to equal five shekels.

Nowadays the first-born may take the place of a Levite (if none is present) on the occasions when the hands of the Cohen have to be washed before the *duchaning*, the priestly benediction.

Bar-Mitzvah/Bat-Mitzvah

CONTRARY to popular belief, the custom of celebrating a barmitzvah with any kind of festivity is of comparatively recent origin.

The first reference to any celebration appears in the legal compendium, the Orach Chayim (225), where it is stated that a father is duty-bound to make a festive meal *(seudat mitzva)* on the day his son becomes thirteen, similar to the obligation to arrange a *seuda* on the day of one's wedding.

The earliest mention of thirteen as being the age a boy becomes barmitzvah (literally, a "son of the commandment") is made in the Mishna — "...at thirteen for the fulfilment of the commandments..." (Avot 5) — where various important landmarks in the life of a Jew are listed.

The boy — who on this day reaches his religious and halachic majority — is henceforth responsible for his own actions and is subject to the same obligations and privileges as an adult regarding the observance of the commandments.

He is initiated into the ranks of the community by fulfilling two mitzvot from which, as a minor, he was previously barred — that of putting on (or "laying") tefillin during week-day morning prayers and of being called up to the reading of the Law *(aliya la'torah)* in the synagogue.

A barmitzvah boy is called up to the Torah on a Monday or a Thursday after he has reached thirteen years and a day, and then again on the following Shabbat to read (if possible) the sidra and haftara (the section from the Prophets). And if he is able, he should be encouraged to conduct the service in order to demonstrate to the wider community his acceptance as an adult member of *K'lal Yisrael,* the totality of Jewry.

Immediately after the boy has been called up, his father pronounces the blessing, *baruch sheptarani me'onsho shel zeh,* "Blessed is He who has now freed me from the responsibility of this one."

The modish custom of arranging lavish and ostentatious celebrations has no basis whatever in Jewish tradition — and is even against Jewish law and ethics. All that is required, says the Maharshal, Rabbi Shlomo Luria (1510-1573), is a modest festive meal on the day the boy is obliged to put on his tefillin. During the meal it is customary for the boy to give a short discourse (pilpul) which includes an halachic topic.

Sephardim give particular emphasis to this custom and term the ceremony "entering the minyan." Now the young man may be included as one of the ten to form a quorum (minyan) needed to qualify as a "congregation" for religious services, and he may also be counted as one of three for the purpose of having a *mezuman* to recite grace after meals.

The tefillin are two box-like containers *(batim)* made of leather and containing the four references to this religious appurtenance mentioned in the Torah, written by a scribe on specially prepared parchment.

The box for the head *(shel rosh)* has four separate compartments for each of the biblical references, while the one attached to the arm *(shel yad)* has only one compartment containing all four quotations on a single piece of parchment.

One explanation for this is that the head, the seat of the brain, allows for people to hold differing opinions and outlooks; the *shel rosh* therefore has separate sections. However, when it comes to action — work of the hand — the community is commanded to be united, symbolised by the single section of the *shel yad.*

Judaism accepts that girls mature sooner than boys and are therefore obliged to begin their religious observances at an earlier age. The bat-mitzvah ceremony has gained in popularity and the girl undergoes a special course of training aimed at equipping her for the role of practising Jewess and future wife and mother.

Youngsters today have a new and memorable way of celebrating their religious majority. Special weekday ceremonies are arranged at the Western Wall in Jerusalem during which presentations are made to the celebrants, leaving an indelible imprint in the minds of all present.

The prayer for this event ends with the words, "...Save me from temptation, so that I may observe Thy holy Torah, and those precepts on which human happiness and eternal life depend. Thus I will throughout the days of my pilgrimage on earth trustfully and gladly proclaim: 'Hear, O Israel, The Lord is our God, the Lord is One!'"

Jewish Education

THE IMPORTANCE of education is paramount in Judaism. The building of the sanctuary was certainly of great consequence to the Children of Israel, but the Talmud nevertheless rules, "Children who attend school are not to be removed from the study of the Torah even for the building of the sanctuary" (Shabbat 119). So, throughout Jewish history, parents have made sacrifices to ensure that their children have received a good education.

The obligation to educate one's children is addressed in the Torah to the parent, as stated in the first passage of the Shema — *v'shinantam l'vanecha*, "and you shall teach them diligently to your children" (Deuteronomy 6). But this was not always possible since sometimes the child was an orphan, and the first-century Rabbi Yehoshua ben Gamla ordained that the education of children was to be a communal responsibility.

The Talmud discusses the question, which is of greater importance, study or action, and unanimously concludes that education and knowledge have priority, since they teach a person the correct manner of action and observance (Kiddushin 40). Ignorance has always been frowned upon in Judaism: an *am ha'aretz* (a "person of the soil", an ignoramus) was considered the lowest category of individual in the community.

Certainly, the age of barmitzvah or batmitzvah is no time to finish one's Jewish education. It is, in fact, the signal for further study in a more serious vein, now that one is obliged to fulfil one's religious obligations with a fuller understanding and appreciation of their purpose.

The Hebrew word for education is *chinuch* ("consecration"), aimed at teaching a child not merely how to make a living, but how to live. Parents who see education only as a means to ensure a reasonable livelihood or a successful career for their children are providing but a fraction of the total education called for by Jewish tradition.

"Train a child in the way he should go, and even when he is old he will not depart from it," declares Proverbs.

The proper purpose of education is to instil into a child's mind the ethical and moral values of Judaism; the active observance of the mitzvot through knowledge of the sources; a strong sense of identification with the Jewish people and Eretz Yisrael together with concern for all mankind.

Jointly with these studies is that part of education which will later enable the child to engage in a suitable trade or profession, so that reliance on charity is ruled out. The talmudic sages in fact state that "a father is obliged to teach his son a skill" in order to earn a dignified livelihood, but it adds that "one should always teach one's son a clean and easy trade" (Berachot 63).

Parental example does much to mould the character of a child, who is told by Solomon, "obey the instruction of your father and forsake not the teaching of your mother" (Proverbs 1); yet "the beginning of wisdom is the fear of the Lord."

The real blueprint for Jewish education can be found in the *Shema*. Were these few verses to be strictly observed, there would be no such thing as a generation gap between parents and children. By "communi-

cating" with one's children, whether at home, when strolling together, coming home at night or starting the day, one breaks down the barriers and, at the same time, nurtures respect, *derech eretz,* for one's elders.

Today as never before it is imperative to know the answers to the many questions one will be asked in later years by non-Jewish friends and colleagues. Any attack on Jewry, Judaism or Israel has to be countered with the true facts and figures, so that the reply is given with confidence and is forceful enough to have the desired effect. The few hours spent in the synagogue Hebrew class until barmitzvah or batmitzvah age are totally insufficient to arm the child with that knowledge which is essential if he or she is to live and behave as a good Jew and good citizen.

The answer is, of course, the Jewish day school, where children are moulded into learned Jews, giving them a thorough understanding of Judaism combined with a good secular education, creating a synthesis of mature knowledge and equipping them to meet the challenges of everyday living.

Chinuch means "upbringing" as well as "dedication" (both are derived from the same root). To be an educated person implies more than just being knowledgeable; it also connotes a person who combines breeding with dedication towards a life based on Torah principles and an understanding of the true aims of his religion.

"Whoever has a son occupying himself in the study of the Torah," says the Midrash (Bereshit Rabbah 49:4), "is as though he never dies."

Study

LONG AGO it was said, "An ignorant person cannot be pious; one who is bashful cannot learn (he is afraid or ashamed to ask); he who is irritable and impatient cannot teach" (Avot 2).

Study and learning have always been the cornerstone of Judaism. When the Children of Israel accepted the Torah at Sinai, it was given to them only when they called out, *"Na'aseh v'nishma,"* we shall do and we shall understand. Since that momentous event, knowing and understanding have been central to Jewish living.

From that very first "Book," the Torah, the cultural history of the Jewish people can be traced through books. The Bible, the Talmud (Mishna and Gemara), the prayer book (Siddur), the commentaries of Maimonides and Rashi, the Shulchan Aruch and the Zohar are but a few of the thousands of volumes that serve as signposts and milestones on the long journey of the Jewish people.

To understand the relevance of Judaism, it is essential to study the vast sea of literature and to continue to do so throughout life. The sages understood this when they taught: "He who does not increase his knowledge, decreases it" (Avot 1).

The same Mishna warns about procrastination by declaring, "Do not say 'when I have leisure I shall study'; perhaps you will never have leisure" (Avot 2). Regular study and fixed times for learning are essential if one wishes to advance one's knowledge.

There is a trend today for youngsters to spend a year or so at yeshiva or seminary before starting university or entering a trade or profession. In this way they are able to concentrate on their Jewish studies without any outside interruption or influence.

Of even greater benefit to them is a period of study in Israel, where the *ruach* and *hashkafah,* the atmosphere and outlook, are bound to influence their future life-styles and equip them with a sound Jewish education necessary for all aspects of life.

We are advised to "know what to answer" (Avot 2) to those who question or challenge the Jewish faith and the Land of Israel. The ability to answer correctly and convincingly requires a thorough knowledge which can be acquired only through consistent study.

Some people frown on further Jewish study with the comment, "He doesn't need it, he's not going to be a rabbi." But the Talmud remarked, "Torah study is valued as much as all the other mitzvot combined" (Peah 1), because the rabbis realised that the unending pursuit of God's teachings will result in the refinement of man, together with contentment and peace of mind.

More recently, the late Chief Rabbi of Israel, Avraham Yitzchak Kook, put it another way: "The main aim of study is to mould man into his civilised form . . . Man is civilised if he acts justly and honestly; to educate man to live in that framework is the supreme aim of Jewish religious study.

"The surest way to achieve this aim is not through an ethics-divorced religion, but through a thorough religious grounding. Without God and religion, any system of ethical education will lack a solid base and constitute an unreliable instrument for civilising man" (Igrot Ha'reiyah).

The synthesis of Torah study and secular study brings about the ideal Jew, one which the Yiddish expression describes as living *zu Got un zu Lat,* "for God and for people." The teacher and writer Rabbi Samson Raphael Hirsch (1808-1888) wrote: "Give your children a well-balanced education in *all* aspects.

"Try to apply the ancient principle which ties religious and secular education closely together and makes one conditional on the other. . . . For the field of Jewish learning is not isolated from nature, history or real life. These two components of education, Torah and general studies, strengthen and support each other" (Judaism Eternal, Volume 1).

The Jewish future lies in Jewish study. More Jewish books should be in more Jewish homes. Learning must become a respected communal commitment. Honour is due no less to scholars, teachers and spiritual leaders than to philanthropists, because, as the Talmud observes, "the learned increase peace and happiness in the world" (Berachot 84).

Visiting the Sick

JUDAISM is concerned about the sanctity of life and stresses that it is the Jew's duty to look after his physical well-being. "And you shall take good care of your bodies," the Torah proclaims in Deuteronomy.

In order to lead a useful and purposeful life, it is essential to remain healthy and to take every possible precaution to be fit and well. The Shulchan Aruch includes rules governing the proper care of the body through cleanliness, diet and habits and cautions against anything that might constitute a danger to health or life. The Talmud says that exercise and physical training are among the skills a parent is obliged to teach his child (Kiddushin 30).

Even with the best care and attention, however, one is likely to suffer illness or disability at some time in one's life. At such times the Talmud has advice to give. "A learned man," say the rabbis in tractate Sanhedrin, "should not live in a city where there is no physician."

From the passage, "And he must cure him" (Exodus 21), we learn that God has granted the doctor permission to cure the patient (Baba Kama 85); and we are told to "ask the patient, not the doctor" when it comes to inquiring about the condition of the afflicted (Yoma 83).

"All aches, but not heartache," stated the Talmud in a reference to worry and stress. But the main concern in Judaism is the preservation of human life and one is required to disregard virtually any law that conflicts with health and life.

All the Shabbat laws, for example, may be suspended in order to safeguard the health of an individual, coming under the Hebrew term, *pikuach nefesh,* "a life in danger." This principle is derived from the verse in Leviticus, "You shall therefore keep my statutes ... which if a man shall do, he shall live by them." To which the rabbis added: "Live by them, and not die by them."

Psychology has a part to play in the therapy and healing of a sick person. Knowing that others care for you facilitates recovery. Imitation of God's ways is a primary goal of religion and one of the cardinal commandments of Judaism is *bikkur cholim* (visiting the sick), following the example set by God when he visited Abraham during his illness.

Responsibility towards the sick has always been at the forefront of Jewish concern. Special bikkur cholim societies exist in most communities and regular visits are made to those who are unwell; in addition, financial help and other practical aid is given where necessary.

A rigid code of conduct is demanded of the visitor which includes cheerful conversation, not staying too long or visiting when a patient is in great pain, and leaving with a brief prayer and a wish for the patient's full and speedy recovery.

During the weekday amida, which is recited three times a day, a prayer is included for the healing of the sick; special provision is made to insert an individual plea for a specific patient. On Shabbat and festivals prayers for the sick may be recited during the reading of the Law.

Sincerity in prayer is always essential, but never more so than when pleading for the sick. This is illustrated by a story told of the Chasidic Lubliner Rebbe (known as the Yud), who became dangerously ill.

The inhabitants of his town proclaimed a day of fasting and prayer for his speedy recovery. A villager went to town and was spotted at an inn by several townsfolk, who told him that drinking was forbidden for the day on account of the Rebbe's illness.

The villager immediately rushed to the synagogue and prayed: "O Lord, please cure the holy rabbi, so that I may have my drink." Soon after, the Rebbe began to recover and said: "The prayer of the villager was more acceptable than any of yours. His plea expressed the greatest longing and the most sincere supplication for my prompt recovery."

Music as an aid to healing goes back to the time when David played the harp for Saul; today it is considered of great therapeutic value. To Jews this is nothing new.

Through music and song one was elevated to a state of sublime serenity, at one with the Almighty and at the threshold of spiritual domains, bringing peace and joy to both performer and listener. The psalms, the chants, the sacred musical service, all brought about inner peace and psychic tranquillity to those who participated.

Music changes the mood and feelings of a person and reaches the very core of his being. That is the meaning of King David's words, *kol atzmotai tomarna* (all my bones speak) — that music and song bring a person nearer to God, giving hope to the sick and at the same time acting as a balm to pain or disability.

Maimonides once declared: "One who suffers from melancholia and depression can sometimes rid himself of it by listening to singing and instrumental music ... to enliven the mind and dissipate gloomy moods.

"The purpose of all this is to restore the healthful condition of the body. But the real object in maintaining the body in good health is to acquire wisdom" (commentary to the Mishna).

Old Age

THE AGED in Judaism have a special claim for respect and honour. Says the Torah: "You shall rise before the grey head and honour the face of the old man" (Leviticus 19).

The external signs of old age, adds the Midrash, came into the world only because Abraham asked for this recognition. "Without the sign of a white beard, how will people know to honour a father before a son?"

Yet there is more to recognition of old age than mere grey hairs. "With the aged comes wisdom, and with length of days comes understanding" (Job 12).

The experiences of the elderly, the landmarks and highlights of their lives, add a new dimension to the education of the young. Not only through photographs and mementos, but also through the voices of the elderly, family history takes on a wider perspective.

It is recognised today that retirement can create many problems. Acknowledging this fact, the Talmud long ago declared: "The ignorant and untutored find that their minds become confused and bewildered as they grow older. But not so with scholars and students. As they grow older, their minds attain a new serenity and an inner peace" (Kinnim 3).

The person who has maintained an interest in study and culture throughout his life finds that, in later years, the steady broadening of knowledge and understanding has led to the attainment of wisdom and contentment. A life conducted along truly Jewish lines is, say the rabbis, a virtual guarantee for longevity.

In reply to the questions, "By virtue of what actions have you reached such a good old age?" or "To what do you ascribe your longevity?" Rabbi Zakkai replied: "I have never given an abusive attribute to any fellow, nor have I omitted to recite Kiddush on Shabbat."

Rabbi Nechunia ben HaKaneh stated: "Never in my life have I sought respect and honour through the degradation of my fellow ... and I have been generous with my money." Rabbi Nechunia the Great similarly asserted: "I have not insisted on retribution when wronged and I have been charitable" (Megila 27-28).

The Torah promises long life as a reward for a number of actions. In the Ten Commandments, for example, if one honours one's parents, "... your days may be prolonged and it may be well with thee" (Deuteronomy 5). And in the case of a mother bird and its offspring in a nest, one is obliged to let the mother go free, "... in order that it shall be well with you and you will prolong your life."

The Shema states that the crowning reward for adherence and commitment to God and His mitzvot is "... so that your days and the days of your children may be multiplied, in the land which the Lord swore unto your fathers to give them" (Deuteronomy 11).

Judaism acknowledges — in the form of prayer — that a life led according to precepts of the Torah is one worthy of reward. As the evening service puts it, *ki heim chayeinu v'orech yameinu*, the Torah and the commandments, the judgements and the laws, are "our life and the length of our days."

The late Rabbi Dr Elie Munk, in his "The World of Prayer," wrote: "The living human being is an indivisible entity. As the state of the body has its profound effects on the activity of mind and soul, thus the operations of the soul in turn influence the body.

"This, indeed, is the wonderful greatness of Judaism — that the hallowing of the soul, the express aim of the law, also guarantees as a consequence the health of the body. He who hallows his life thereby protects and prolongs it."

Moses taught us that what counts is not really the number of years we spend on earth, but rather what we put into, and make of, every day we live. "Teach us to number our days that we may get us a heart of wisdom."

It is appropriate that this psalm should be included in the Shabbat and festival morning liturgy when we have maximum time to contemplate on the meaning of time. Just as we sanctify Shabbat and the festivals and divide them into two equal parts — for the service of God and for our own personal needs and enjoyment — so should we sanctify our everyday lives for service to God and man.

The Book of Ecclesiastes concludes with a reminder that the greatest mitzva is the real enjoyment of life, because if we cherish life, we express our gratitude to God, who gives life. One should seek happiness before old age sets in, says Kohelet, since disability and weakness will not allow full enjoyment of God's creation and works.

לְמַעַן יִרְבּוּ יְמֵיכֶם

Faith

THE ENTIRE history of the Jewish people is built around acts of faith — the Patriachs' belief in one God; the Israelites' trust in "the Lord and in Moses, His servant" at the time of the Exodus; and their act of faith during the Revelation at Sinai. In our own time, the inmates of the concentration camps sang *ani ma'amin,* "I believe in perfect faith," even as they entered the gas chambers.

Faith is the first and cardinal principle in Judaism: a firm belief in the course prescribed by God for the good of mankind through the code of the Torah. Faith in Judaism is inseparable from action and observance.

The Hebrew for faith, *emuna,* is derived from the same root as *uman,* a craftsman, one who is an expert in his trade, though he began with a leaning towards that craft. Similarly, the Jew must begin with a firm hold on faith which he is prepared to nurture so as to acquire the necessary skills to live as a Jew.

The founder of the Lubavitch movement, the Ladiyer Rebbe, was once imprisoned in Czarist Russia on a false charge. Encountering the saintly rabbi, the prison warden one day asked him, "How was it that after Adam had eaten the apple from the Tree of Knowledge in the Garden of Eden, God called out: 'Where are you?' Did not God, who knows everything, know where Adam was?"

Without hesitation, the rabbi replied: "Of course God knew where Adam was. But he wanted to know if Adam — man — knew where *He* was!" Faith teaches man how to find his place, through the qualities of truth, honesty and sincerity, which are the essence of righteousness.

The Talmud remarks (Makkot 24) that "613 precepts were transmitted to Moses. Then came Habakkuk, who reduced them all to one principle, as it is said, 'The righteous man shall live by his faith.' "

The precepts are there to guide one through life, but a person needs faith in the outcome of those precepts during the weighty journey to his salvation. As the Rabbi of Radin, the Chafetz Chayim, put it: "For those with faith there are no questions, and for those without faith there are no answers."

Faith provides the capacity to meet the challenges of life. Without it a person and a nation plunge into darkness and despair. Implored the Psalmist: "Help us, O Lord, when faith has vanished from mankind" (Psalm 2).

Emuna has another meaning, as evidenced in Exodus 17:12 — "steady," "steadfastness." This sums up the whole notion of faith — that firmness and resolution bring progress and prosperity. This was the faith first mentioned in the Bible about Abraham, "And he had faith in the Lord and he accounted it to him for righteousness" (Genesis 15).

Yet another derivation of the word *emuna* is contained in the acclamation Amen which, uttered after hearing a blessing, suggests faith in the Giver of blessings. "Amen" expresses a belief that the world has a Creator and that the Torah is the God-given guide to man. Said Israel: "All that the Lord has spoken we will do and obey."

In his book, "Man Is Not Alone," the late Professor Abraham Heschel dealt with the meaning of faith. "To have faith," he wrote, "is to perceive the wonder that is here, and to be stirred by the desire to integrate the self into the holy order of living.

"Faith does not detach man from thinking, it does not suspend reason. It is opposed not to knowledge, but to indifferent aloofness to the essence of living . . .

"Faith is an awareness of divine mutuality and companionship, a form of communion between God and man. Faith is the insight that life is not a self-maintaining, private affair, not a chaos of whims and instincts, but an inspiration, a way, not a refuge.

"Faith is real only when it is not one-sided, but reciprocal. Man can rely on God, if God can rely on man."

King David (Psalm 92) pointed out that when things are dark and dreary, it is time to have faith. The Thirteen Principles of Faith by the twelfth-century physician and philosopher, Maimonides, provided just such a formula for difficult times.

Today they are included in the prayer book, after the morning service. They can also be found, in poetical form, in the well-known Yigdal prayer at the beginning of the Siddur, written by Daniel ben Yehuda of Rome around the year 1300.

Prebuilt structure

Prayer

THE SECOND paragraph of the Shema states: "To love the Lord your God and to serve Him with all your heart." The rabbis of the Talmud taught that service of the heart means prayer (Ta'anit 2).

Such importance is attached to prayer that an entire tractate of the Talmud, Berachot, is devoted to the subject. In it are discussed the time, place, occasions, content and form of prayer.

Through the details described therein prayer emerges as the bridge between earth and heaven, linking man's feelings — elation and depression, hope and despair — with the Creator. In gratitude and wonder, supplication and penitence, pleasure and affliction we pronounce our deepest emotions to God. Prayer is not the invention of religious leaders; it has been with man since Creation itself.

The Book of Genesis shows the three Patriarchs approaching prayer from the standpoint of their individual personalities. Abraham undertook a task with the least possible delay, with *z'rizut* (alertness), and found that the best time for prayer was early in the morning, before daily routine commenced.

Isaac saw that one needed to have a break from the day's tasks, to refreshen and revitalise oneself in order to carry on the complete day's duties. So he "meditated in the field" and prayed at sunset.

Jacob, on the other hand, found that, when alone and relaxed at night, he could best pour out his heart in prayer. So the three daily prayers of *shacharit* (morning), *mincha* (after-noon) and *ma'ariv* (evening) were instituted.

Rabbi Yehuda Halevi (1095-1150), in his "Kuzari," stated that the three periods of prayer should constitute the most fruitful and elevated part of the day and that one should look forward to the opportunity of communion with God. He cautioned, however, against praying in a mechanical way, without thought or understanding of the words being said.

He added that prayer was for the soul what food was for the body. The benefit of one prayer lasted until the next, just as the strength gained from one meal sufficed to carry one over to the next.

Prayers may be divided into four categories: *beracha* — blessing, *tehila* — praise, *bakasha* — petition, and *todah* — thanks. Whether one prays by oneself or with a congregation, the prayers are generally worded in the plural, because "a person should always associate himself with the congregation and never exclude himself from the general body of the community" (Talmud, tractate Berachot 29 and 49).

A Chasidic story is told of an uneducated Jew who was lost in the woods. As nightfall approached, his anxiety grew and he addressed himself to the Almighty: "Dear God, I do not know how to pray, but I do remember the *aleph bet*. I shall recite the letters of the alphabet a few times and you put them together in the right way. And please lead me out of this wood."

While praying, one is obliged to concentrate on the words being recited, banishing all other thoughts. This concept is known as *kavana*, concentration and devotion, which the rabbis rule refers to the observance of every mitzva.

Nor are our obligations fulfilled by mere performance. The Maharal of Prague (1512-1609) stated that the word *tefila* (prayer) is derived from the same root as meditation: "Prayer without *kavana* is like a body without a soul."

The famous Berditchever Rebbe once walked over to a group of his Chasidim after the Amidah prayer, shook hands with them and greeted them with "Shalom Aleichem." The congregants looked surprised at this unexpected gesture and the Rebbe explained: "I saluted you in this way because I could read from your expressions that you had no idea of the meaning of the words you were reciting. Rather were you thinking of the grain market in Odessa or the woollen market in Lodz. Now that you have returned from such a long journey, I extend to you a welcome back."

The direction one faces during prayer is discussed in the Talmud, which states: "Let him who prays cast his eyes downward, but turn his heart upwards." And with Eretz Yisrael being at the heart of the Jewish people, it adds:

"A Jew outside the Land of Israel wishing to pray turns his heart towards the Land of Israel. If he is in the land, he turns his heart towards Jerusalem. If he is in Jerusalem, he turns his heart towards the Holy of Holies. If he is in the Holy of Holies, he turns his heart towards the Holy Ark. Thus, all Jews praying are directing their hearts towards one place."

Mourning

DURING THE period of national mourning commemorating the destruction of the Temples it is not inappropriate to discuss personal mourning in the life of the Jew.

"It is better to go to the house of mourning than to go to the house of feasting," says Ecclesiastes, for a house of mourning induces humility, whereas a place of feasting encourages pride and forgetfulness of the purpose of life.

The Torah first refers to the custom of mourning for the passing of a near relative in connection with Abraham's grief on the death of Sarah (Genesis 23), and the period of seven days' mourning (shiva) was observed by Joseph following the death of Jacob: "And he made a mourning for his father seven days" (Genesis 50).

Over the centuries the rabbis have shifted the centre of concern from the unknown and mysterious aura of death to the welfare of the living. Although every possible honour must be accorded the deceased, providing comfort and hope for the mourners is of greater importance.

Excessive grief is not permitted, however. The Talmud states: "Three days for weeping, seven for lamenting, and thirty for abstaining from a haircut and pressed clothes" (Moed Kattan 27).

Such acts as those which reflect respect and devotion for the departed help to fill in the long hours of the shiva. Time should be spent in prayer, in studying appropriate laws and customs and in discussing the merits of the deceased with family and friends who come to bring comfort during this difficult period.

So strong is the holiness and serenity of the Sabbath or festival day that the mourning practices associated with the shiva are suspended on these days and are completely terminated on the eve of a festival.

Many of the mourning customs stem from instructions given by God to the prophet Ezekiel after the death of his wife. The first meal, seudat havra'a, is eaten on one's return from the cemetery, prepared and brought in by neighbours; leather shoes may not be worn during the shiva period; and the mourner is not permitted to greet anyone. During this period one is encouraged to make every effort to return slowly to normal day-to-day activity.

The four distinct periods of mourning prescribed by Jewish law are designed to diminish the intensity of grief. They are known as aninut (between death and burial), shiva (seven), sheloshim (thirty) and aveilut (mourning).

The aveilut period lasts for eleven months after the sheloshim period of thirty days when, following the death of a parent, one may not take part in or attend any form of entertainment. A single person may, however, marry, in a simple ceremony, since the biblical commandment of marriage overrides the laws of mourning. The rabbis rule that it is forbidden to grieve over the loss of a near one for longer than a year.

The mitzva of comforting the mourner (nichum aveilim) is incumbent only after the burial, and the Talmud adds that silence in a house of mourning is praiseworthy. The Bible gives graphic descriptions of consolation on a number of occasions — Jacob being comforted by his children (Genesis 37), David consoling Bathsheba (II Samuel 12) — but the most vivid is that in the Book of Job (2:11) from whose text the sages

deduced that a visitor should not speak before the mourner has spoken and that he should not stay longer than necessary.

Nor is it essential to converse at all if this causes embarrassment to either visitor or mourner. The mere presence of a visitor is enough to bring consolation to the bereaved.

Tradition provides the visitor with a meaningful formula addressed to mourners before leaving: "May God console you along with the other mourners of Zion and Jerusalem." The Jewish homeland, the heart of the Jewish people, is never forgotten, even at times of intimate personal grief.

The erection of a tombstone dates back to the times of the Patriarchs as an act of reverence and respect for the deceased. The monument constructed by Jacob over Rachel's grave has been one of the holiest places in Eretz Yisrael throughout the centuries. Yad Avshalom (Absalom's monument) in Jerusalem was erected by Absalom himself since he had no son to preserve his memory.

In Israel it is customary to erect a tombstone immediately after the sheloshim period, but elsewhere one usually waits until the year of mourning is over on the grounds that the dead are not forgotten within the first year.

The custom of "consecrating" a tombstone is a contemporary innovation and has no basis in halacha. The occasion, admittedly, provides another opportunity to pay tribute to the deceased, but the placing of a stone and the recitation of suitable Psalms are all that is necessary.

Tombstones originally bore brief inscriptions giving the name of the deceased and that of the father. Later, it was customary to include biblical quotations and words of praise, mainly to impress on the living the virtues of the departed in the hope that their example might be followed.

The talmudic scholar, Rabbi Yehonatan Eibeschutz (1690-1764), wrote his own epitaph: "Every passer-by should see what is engraved here. The man who stood as a model ... returned to dust. Pray, take it to heart to sincerely repent .. learn to despise vain glory and to flee from it."

Giving a Name

WHAT TREMENDOUS joy and delight are brought to parents and family on the birth of a child! Discussions immediately take place regarding the naming of the new-born infant.

Indeed, the parents have probably spent hours on the choice of a name even before the birth itself. After all, the child will carry the name given to it through life — and even after.

One's Hebrew name is used on all legal Jewish documents, such as the marriage document (the ketuba), in offering prayers for health, on being called up to the reading of the Law, on tombstones and in memorial prayers recited on appropriate occasions during the year.

One often hears the remark, "What's in a name?" Jewish tradition, in fact, attaches great significance to a name and to the reputation associated with it. The Talmud states, for example, that Rabbi Meir was able to establish the true character of a person by analysing his name (Yoma 83).

In older editions of the Siddur, at the end of the daily Amida prayer, an alphabetical list of biblical names is given. An appropriate one is to be selected by the worshipper in order to remind him (or her) of the significance of his own name. It is clear from this that women are also expected to recite prayers from the morning service.

A girl is often given a name sooner than a boy, since the father is able to do this on any day on which the Torah is read. A boy, on the other hand, is named at his *brit* (circumcision), just as Abraham was named by God at the time of the covenant (Genesis 17) — and the same applied to his son, Isaac.

It is customary (though not, of course, mandatory) to name a child after a deceased relative in order to honour him or her and to perpetuate the memory of that person. Bearing the name of an illustrious forebear should act as a reminder of his good deeds and good name.

Judaism teaches that a good name and reputation are the apex of a person's achievements. The Ethics of the Fathers (4:17) declare: "Rabbi

Simeon said, 'There are three crowns: the crown of the Torah, the crown of priesthood and the crown of royalty; but the crown of a good name excels them all.'"

Our sages teach that every person has, in fact, three names: one given by parents, one given by friends, and one given — and made — by oneself (Kohelet Rabbah 7:3). The same source quotes Rabbi Shimon bar Yochai as saying: "More beloved by God than the ark of the covenant is a good name."

It is only in the past 200 years or so that surnames or family names, which become obligatory by law, were introduced among Jews in most parts of Europe. The early settlers in England, in the twelfth century, were French-speaking Jews who used such patronyms as Isaac or Joseph, since these were popular in France at the time.

Until then, people were identified by their own name and that of their father, such as Yochanan ben Zakai or Shlomo ibn Gavirol.

When surnames were adopted, they were, in the main, biblical names, such as Cohen, Levi, Aarons and Abrahams. Subsequently, names became associated with places where one lived — Berliner, Lemberger, Englander. Others took on a name illustrating their occupation, such as Schneider, Kaufmann and Goldschmidt.

In modern Israel it has become commonplace to name children after flowers — Shoshana, Hadassah — or other beautiful objects of nature. Surnames are also being Hebraised: Goldberg becomes Har-Zahav, Stein becomes Avni, Goldstone becomes Even-Paz.

A custom derived from the Talmud (Rosh Hashana 16), to give someone an additional name when dangerously ill, is meant "to avert the evil decree in heaven." The names, usually given in the framework of a special prayer for the sick, are Chaim ("life") or Refael ("God will heal") for a male, and Chaya ("lively") for a female. This practice is known as *shinui hashem* (change of name).

An adopted child may be named as the son or daughter of the adoptive parent, but if the adoptive father is a Cohen or Levite, the child does not assume that title. Where a Hebrew name is given following a conversion, the person adopting Judaism becomes the son or daughter of the first Jew, Abraham.

Various customs regarding names are still prevalent today. Thus, in certain circles, one is not encouraged to marry a girl who has the same Hebrew name as one's mother, so that, if necessary, one of them should change her name (Sefer Chasidim 23).

Contractions or abbreviations of names which describe a communal position are not uncommon. The name Katz stands for *kohen tzedek* (a priest), Shatz for *sheliach tzibur* (a reader or cantor), Segal for *s'gan Levi* (deputy Levite).

"A good name," says Ecclesiastes, "is better than precious oil." Jacob's name was changed to Israel because he had "striven with beings divine and human, and prevailed."

Circumcision

OF ALL THE 613 commandments in the Torah, only three were designated as "signs" between God and man: Shabbat, tefilin (phylacteries) and brit mila (circumcision).

The "sign" of the brit demonstrates that although we are the creation of the Almighty, He desires that we ourselves do something to make us perfect in body and mind. We thereby play a part in that perfection through the act of circumcision. Abram's name became "complete" — being changed to Abraham — only after his circumcision.

A brit's importance can be gauged by the fact that Sabbath and even Yom Kippur laws are suspended if either coincides with the eighth day after the baby's birth. Circumcision was the first mitzva given to the progenitor of the Jewish people, before the rest of the Torah was disclosed.

From the biblical words, "And Abraham circumcised his son Isaac when he was eight days old, as God had commanded him," the rabbis taught that it is a father's duty to perform the brit (though he may delegate the responsibility) and that the ceremony has to take place on the eighth day. Only for health reasons may a brit be postponed beyond the eighth day.

The Chasidic Rebbe of Belz said: "The brit is performed on the eighth day to teach us that when we visit someone's home, we should first greet the lady of the house and then turn our attention to the master. The child is given an opportunity first to welcome the Sabbath Bride before being initiated into the company of the Master."

For the ceremony itself it is preferable to have a minyan, a quorum of ten males, since this enhances the observance of the mitzva. Where this is not possible, however, the mohel may carry out the circumcision in the presence of the father alone. The mohel is a pious and observant Jew thoroughly conversant with the laws of circumcision, as spelled out in the Shulchan Aruch (the code of Jewish law), and is trained over a long period in the most advanced techniques of surgical hygiene.

A brit should always take place during the day, preferably early in the morning, in keeping with the talmudic maxim z'reezim u'makdeemim, the diligent hasten to perform a mitzva.

The ceremony is initiated by a husband and wife team, known as the kvater and kvateren. The latter takes the child from the mother and passes him to the kvater, who in turn hands him to the father, now standing in front of the chair where the brit will take place.

It has been suggested that the name kvater originates from adding the Hebrew prefix "k—" to the Yiddish vater, "father," so that the word came to mean "like a father." The real father appoints a deputy since he himself has no heart to perform this ceremony on his own child, and the kvater, as it were, commences the proceedings.

When the child is carried into the room, all present proclaim, baruch ha-ba, blessed is he who comes. The commentator Abudraham suggests that since the numerical value of the word haba is eight, we mean: "Blessed is the one who arrives to be circumcised on the eighth day."

Commenting on the reason for the special chair known as the Chair of Elijah (kissei shel Eliyahu), he asserts that the prophet Elijah was the personification of absolute faith. Elijah's insistence on the ethical and spiritual values of monotheism served to present him as the embodiment of the true and absolute Jewish spirit. Having complained to God that Israel had forsaken the ritual of circumcision (I Kings 19), Elijah was ordered to witness the loyalty of Israel by being present at every brit.

The person who holds the child during the ceremony is called the sandek (a Greek term meaning "godfather"). A commentary on Genesis 50:23 states that Joseph acted in that capacity for one of his grandsons.

Immediately after the brit the father recites the blessing for this mitzva, intended as a prayer of thanksgiving for having been blessed with a son and for having entered him into the Covenant of Abraham. The assembled guests respond with their own prayer: "As the infant entered the covenant, so may he enter the study of the Torah, into marriage and into the performance of good deeds."

This is based on the talmudic ruling that it is a father's duty to educate his son, to secure a good wife for him and to lead him in the path of righteousness. Just as the ritual has been carried out and the child has joined the family of the Jewish people with such simplicity, so may other milestones in his life take place at the right time and with the ease of the brit mila ceremony.

In Israel the blessing recited on all joyous occasions, shehecheyanu, is recited by the father.

In the course of a prayer after the circumcision, the child's name is proclaimed, based on the occasion when Abraham named his son, Isaac (Genesis 21). The ceremony then concludes with a seudat mitzva, a festive meal, which also has its origins in the circumcision of Isaac.

Speech

THE POWER of speech distinguishes man from other living creatures and thus has to be used with great responsibility. "Death and life are in the power of the tongue," says Proverbs.

Both the Mishna and the Talmud are replete with advice regarding the proper use of speech. Shammai's maxim, "Say little and do much" (Avot 1: 15), refers mainly to hospitality and charity, but it can be used generally to good effect. "A man should not speak one thing with his mouth and another with his heart," says the tractate Baba Metzia.

The eleventh-century Spanish philosopher, Bachya ibn Pakuda, summed it up thus: "Reflect further on the benefits God has bestowed on man by the gift of speech and the orderly arrangement of words, whereby he gives expression to what is in his mind and soul and understands the conditions of others.

"The tongue is the heart's pen and the mind's messenger. Lacking speech, there would be no social relations between one person and another; a human being would be like the cattle. Speech makes manifest the superiority of an individual among his fellows."

"Say little and do much"

One of the most important functions of speech is, of course, the part it plays in teaching the Jewish way of life. The talmudist, Nachmanides (1194-1270), wrote from the Holy Land to his eldest son: "Hear, my son, the instruction of your father, and do not forsake the teaching of your mother. Accustom yourself to speak in gentleness to all men at all times."

There is a time to speak and a time to remain silent. "Press your lips together and don't be in a hurry to answer," advises the Talmud (Avodah Zarah 35). "If silence is good for the wise, how much better for fools" (Pesachim 98). And Proverbs adds: "Even a fool, if he remains silent, is thought wise."

The sages have stressed the importance of purity of speech and the Talmud gives several examples of how one should avoid coarse and indecent language.

Rabbi Joshua ben Levi found an allusion to this in the first chapters of Genesis, where God speaks to Noah about the ark and the inclusion "of clean beasts, and of beasts *that are not clean*" (Genesis 7).

A single Hebrew word, *temeia* ("unclean"), could have been used here, but the rabbi says that the circumlocution teaches us that no indecent words should be expressed in our speech.

The Hebrew language, known as *l'shon hakodesh* ("the holy tongue"), is so called, according to Maimonides, because it contains no indecent expressions or words. "It only hints at them, as if to indicate that these things should not be mentioned, and should therefore have no names."

According to the rabbis of the Talmud, the person who speaks Hebrew regularly is assured of a share in the afterlife.

During the weeks of preparation for the High Holy-days, the period of repentance, it is timely to heed the talmudic warning that abusive talk — slander, gossip, lying, flattery and tale-bearing — is responsible for both individual and collective misfortune.

"Our forefathers provoked God in the wilderness ten times, but were ultimately punished for the defamatory gossip voiced by the ten spies on their report of the Holy Land" (Avot d'Rabbi Natan 89).

The Bible does not hide the faults of its personalities. Miriam, Moses' sister, was punished with leprosy because she slandered her brother.

On Yom Kippur we ask God to grant atonement "for the sin which we have committed before Thee by slander." The Chofetz Chayim said: "I have observed that when a doctor wants to determine the condition of a person's health, he examines his tongue.

"It seems to me that the tongue is a most reliable indicator of a person's spiritual health. How one speaks, and the subjects spoken about, are a good indication of the character of that person."

The sins of *lashon hara* and *rechilut,* slander and gossip, are considered to be among the most heinous. As the Midrash has it: "The slanderer speaks in Rome and kills his victim in Syria."

The gossipmonger is worse than a murderer, says the Talmud, since a murderer kills only his victim, while the gossip slays three people — himself, the listener and the one being spoken about.

Three times a day, at the end of each Amida, we are reminded about our speech. We pray: "My God, guard my tongue from evil and my lips from speaking falsehood. Let my soul be silent to those who slander me and let my soul be as the dust to all. . . ."

The Synagogue

THE MISHKAN, the Tabernacle in the wilderness; the *bet hamikdash,* the Temple in Jerusalem; the *bet haknesset,* the synagogue: this is the sequence of special buildings set aside for worship in the history of the Jews.

Since the destruction of the Temple, the synagogue has become the central and most sacred institution in the life of the Jew. Be it a building such as existed in Alexandria in talmudic times — so large that a flag was raised at the appropriate times for all to respond "Amen" — or a tiny shtibl, which can accommodate only a few worshippers, the synagogue was the one place where the Jew could commune with God and find solace and peace in a troubled world.

Since the synagogue was used not only for prayer, but also for study, it became known in Yiddish, and in colloquial English, as shul, from the German word for school, *Schule.* The "Sefer Hamatamim" also points out that the initial letters of the Hebrew *shibchu v'hodu lishmo,* "they offered praises and gave thanks to His name" (from the evening service), make up the word shul.

The design and structure of the synagogue have changed over the years according to communal requirements and architectural taste. But certain basic features have remained the same. The building has always faced towards Jerusalem and the holy ark, which houses the Torah scrolls, is always placed or built into the *mizrach* (eastern) wall.

In the past, the synagogues of the Ashkenazi communities tended to be more opulent and impressive, while those of the Sephardim were of a more modest nature, although no less artistic in design.

Although the main purpose of the synagogue has always been communal devotion and worship, the Hebrew connotation, *bet haknesset,* house of assembly, describes more appropriately the various activities which take place within its precincts. Education of the young, religious instruction for adults, hospitality for the stranger, charity for the poor — all the needs of the community are centred on the synagogue.

It is this power-house of Judaism

"Know before whom you are standing"

which carries the current of our faith into the lives of its members. It is the place to which Jews gravitate to express gratitude in times of joy, and to mourn at those unfortunate times of sadness.

Said King David in Psalm 16: "I have set the Lord *always* before me." In good times and in bad, the synagogue was able to lighten man's load, to bring him close to God, to make him feel, in Jacob's words, that "This is none other than the House of God" (Genesis 28).

The first mention of synagogues is made after the destruction of the First Temple, when the Jews were exiled to Babylon. And it was during the period of the Second Temple that the membership of the Great Assembly *anshei knesset hagedola,* came into being during the era of Ezra the Scribe, following the return of the Jews from the Babylonian exile. The men of the Great Assembly decided on the establishment of buildings in which Jews should pray, on the compilation of orders of services and on the way that these services were to be conducted.

Discussing the verse in Ezekiel 11 "...yet have I been to them as a little sanctuary in the countries where they came," Rabbi Isaac states in the Talmud: "This refers to the synagogues and houses of learning in Babylon" (Megila 29). So the Divine Presence, the *shechina,* was transferred from the Temple in Jerusalem to the "little sanctuary," *mikdash m'at,* the synagogue in exile.

Similarly, after the destruction of the First Temple, many Jews went to live in Egypt, where they, too, built large and beautiful synagogues as so vividly described in the Talmud (Succah 51).

On their return to the Holy Land after the building of the Second Temple, they continued to erect synagogues and to assemble in them for congregational prayers, as they had done in Egypt. The Jerusalem Talmud gives the number of synagogues in Jerusalem alone during that period as 480, in addition to the Temple itself.

From then on, in and out of exile, Jews established synagogues and appointed officials to organise and run the activities that became the focal point of Jewish life.

In difficult times the synagogue was even turned into a place of refuge. During an epidemic in Kovno, the hospitals were filled to capacity with patients. The saintly Rabbi Yisrael Salanter visited every synagogue in the city and declared from the pulpits: "It will please God more to turn the synagogues into hospitals than to conduct services in them."

The synagogue is designed to be the place where young and old find common ground, where brotherhood and warmth prevail. Wherever he may be, the Jew can soon find himself at home in the building on which the spiritual foundation of his Judaism rests.

In his "Laws on Prayer," Maimonides points out that it is a mitzva to proceed to the synagogue quickly and with zeal, as indicated by the verse, "...let us be eager to know the Lord" (Hosea 6). Equally, one should leave the sacred building at a slow, respectful pace.

The Ark and Bimah

THE ENTIRE synagogue is a place of holiness, but the highest degree of sanctity is attached to the ark, the *aron hakodesh,* and its contents.

Wherever a synagogue is situated, the ark is placed against or within the wall which faces toward Jerusalem. Its origin goes back to the wandering of the Israelites in the wilderness, when the Ark of the Covenant, *aron habrit,* was used to house the stone tablets which Moses had received on Sinai and which later stood in the Holy of Holies of the First Temple.

Later, the ark became the receptacle for the Torah scrolls — which have a unique sanctity of their own — and a focal point for prayers of special solemnity and significance. Sephardim call this part of the synagogue *heichal,* the sanctuary, while in the Mishna it is known as *teiva,* a chest or box.

In view of its special status, one is forbidden to sell an ark in order to build a synagogue, though one may sell the seats or the reading desk in order to buy an ark. This is deduced from the talmudic maxim, *ma'alin bakodesh v'lo moridin,* "In matters of holiness one may ascend, but not descend" (Berachot 28).

It is customary not to leave the ark empty, so that on such occasions as Simchat Torah and Hoshana Rabba, when all the scrolls are removed, a lighted candle is placed in the ark, symbolic of the light of the Torah.

The traditional ornamental curtain concealing the doors of the Ashkenazi ark, the *parochet,* derived its name from the curtain which hung in front of the Holy of Holies in the Temple, separating it from the sanctuary (Exodus 26). Sephardi communities place the *parochet* inside the ark, behind the doors.

The Eternal Light, *ner tamid,* which is suspended in front of the ark, is a symbolic reminder of the continually burning menora of the Temple. So many features of the synagogue resemble characteristics of the Temple that it is not surprising the Talmud considers the bet haknesset to be a spiritual replica, a "miniature sanctuary" *(mikdash m'at).*

The *ner tamid* serves to remind the Jew both of God's *shechina,* His presence, in the synagogue and to act with the reverence and respect due to a place of sanctity. At the time of the Tabernacle in the wilderness the Israelites were commanded: ". . . bring thee pure olive oil beaten for the light, to cause the lamp to burn always" (Exodus 27). Candles were later employed and nowadays it is permitted to use an electric bulb.

The everlasting light has become a medium of artistic expression for ornate designs and intricate shapes, symbolising Israel's undying faith and emphasising the notion that "the spirit of man is the lamp of the Lord" (Proverbs 20).

The bima, the elevated platform, is traditionally placed in the centre of the building. Many authorities suggest that this is to remind us of the Tabernacle used during the Israelites' wanderings in the desert, situated in the centre of a square formed by the twelve tribes, with the Divine Presence hovering over it.

Other commentators say that since, according to Jewish tradition, the Temple stood in the centre of the universe — to diffuse its spiritual light to all four corners of the globe — so the bima, for where the Torah is read, stands centrally to enable its message to be conveyed throughout the world

— and, on a smaller scale, equally clearly to every corner of the synagogue.

Since the Torah scroll is the most sacred object in the synagogue, the congregation is required to stand, as a sign of respect, whenever it is raised or removed from the ark. But one may remain seated during the reading of the Torah, as it is read from the elevated bima, which is considered an independent domain, *reshut bifnei atzmo* (Rama, Yoreh Deah 242).

Mention of the bima (also known as *almemar,* from the Arabic for a platform or pulpit), as the lectern for the reading of the Torah is made as early as the fifth century BCE, in the time of Nechemia; and the Talmud records it as being the place from which communal announcements were also made (Succah 51).

Since then a wide range of styles and shapes has characterised this focal point in the synagogue. In Spain it was a wooden structure, supported by columns and reached by a stairway. In Eastern Europe it was usually enclosed by wrought-iron fencing, while in Central Europe it became a roofed-in structure.

In some Orthodox synagogues only parts of the service are conducted from the bima, with the chazan standing for most of the time at a separate reading stand, the *ammud,* to the right of the Ark. This is placed at a lower level, corresponding to the mishnaic maxim, *yored lifnei hateiva,* "Go down before the Ark" (to lead in prayer), and from the verse in Psalm 130, "Out of the depths have I cried unto thee, O Lord."

In Sephardi synagogues the bima is used both for the reading of the Law and for the chazan while conducting services; the table on which the Torah is placed is known as the *teiva.*

The bima in China's Kai-Fung-Fu synagogue, one of the oldest in the world, was designed as a desk with extended sides placed on top of circular platforms. This was particularly suitable when processional circuits were made around the bima — during Succot, with the four species, and on Simchat Torah, with the *hakkafot.*

The Gallery and Appurtenances

MODESTY and refinement have always been the hallmarks of the Jewish woman; they are known in Hebrew by the term *tzniut,* which also implies such virtues as piety, goodness and dignity.

These attributes apply both to the home and to the synagogue. The fact that women take a silent part in public worship is not to be considered derogatory, but rather a tribute to their status: as the conventional code of behaviour weakens, so the need for modesty grows.

Nowhere is this point more clearly emphasised than in the synagogue, during prayer and meditation when, says the Talmud, "our eyes should be turned downward and our hearts upward to our Father in Heaven."

Since Temple times areas allotted for prayer have included a ladies' gallery, or women's court — *ezrat nashim.* The Talmud describes the areas for men and women which were kept separate during the celebrations in the Temple on the second night of Succot. And recent excavations in Israel have revealed that the synagogue of old had galleries on three sides, supported by pillars.

The rabbis have ruled that women are not exempt from prayer, as they are from positive commandments which have a fixed time *(mitzvot asei shehazeman grama),* since prayer is a supplication for Divine mercy applicable at all times. But they do not take an active part in conducting the service.

The separation or partition is also known as a *mechitza,* which need not be a gallery, but can be a screen or latticed division on the same or a slightly raised level, in order to separate the two sections of the synagogue. In modern multi-purpose buildings a mobile structure is often used during services.

Together with the respective positions of the ark and the bima, the requirement for an *ezrat nashim* during services constitutes the only other restriction governing the interior layout of a traditional synagogue.

The Torah being an object of ultimate veneration, Jews have brought to it their outstanding artistic

talent in the form of lavish decorations with which to embellish the scrolls. They come in various shapes and sizes, each according to the craftman's imagination, made out of chased silver or wood.

These items, used purely for religious purposes, are known as *tashmishei kedusha* or, more commonly, *klei kodesh,* and are themselves vested with sanctity. They call to mind similar adornments used in the Tabernacle and the Temple (described in considerable detail in Numbers 3).

Crowning the scroll are two finials — *rimmonim* (pomegranates") — which often include small bells and lion shapes; these are placed on the handles, *atzei chayim,* of the scroll. Alternatively, this takes the form of an actual crown, *keter Torah,* which signifies the majesty of the Divine Law.

The covering of the scroll differs between the Ashkenazi and Sephardi communities. The former is in the style of a silk or velvet mantle, embroidered with such traditional motifs as lions, crowns, the tablets of the Ten Commandments or the Magen David.

The lion represents the tribe of Judah and symbolises strength; the crown denotes the kingship of God; the Magen David, is said to resemble the six-pointed shield of King David.

·Sephardim use a decorated chased metal or embossed leather case, made in a cylindrical fashion and hinged vertically, so that the two halves open like a book, revealing columns of the Torah script. During their public reading of the Law, the Torah remains

in an upright position, making it unnecessary for the case to be removed.

Over the mantle hangs the decorative breastplate, *choshen* or *tzitz,* which relates to the breastplate worn by the High Priest in the Temple, studded with twelve stones to represent the tribes of Israel. This is usually made of silver, and the lower part often includes a space for a plate on which is engraved the name of the Sabbath or festival on which the scroll is being used.

In front of the breastplate, also hanging on a chain over the *atzei chayim,* is the pointer, *yad,* made out of silver or wood and used by the person who reads the Torah to follow the text, since the parchment may not be touched by hand. The pointer, shaped like a small staff, has a narrow end in the form of a clenched fist with the forefinger outstretched.

The scroll is bound together by a wide ribbon, *mappa,* often exquisitely embroidered and presented to the synagogue by the parents of young children whose names and dates of birth, together with biblical quotations or scenes from Jewish life, are depicted on it. This is done to encourage the children to perform miztvot from an early age.

The *klei kodesh* also include the kiddush cup used for the blessing over wine and the spice-box and candle-holder use for havdala at the termination of Shabbat. On weekdays a *tzedaka* box for charitable contributions (in Temple times it provided both for repairs to the building and for help to the poor) is circulated among the worshippers.

The synagogue appurtenances are often presented by members of the congregation who wish to perpetuate the memory of a parent of other relative. By so doing, the donor participates in the mitzva of *hidur,* zeal in religious observance and embellishment of a holy object.

The silversmiths, artists and scribes, in turn, are able to help fulfil the rabbinic injunction: "Prepare a beautiful sefer Torah, written by an able scribe with fine ink, and wrapped in beautiful silk."

The Rabbi, Chazan and Shamash

THE FUNCTIONS of the rabbi or minister have changed considerably over the centuries in accord with the needs and customs of the respective communities.

The rabbis of the talmudic period usually followed other occupations. Hillel, for example, was a woodcutter, Shammai a builder, Joshua a blacksmith, and Chanina a shoemaker. Some of the occupations could be identified by the rabbis' names. Thus, Yochanan Hasandlar was a sandalmaker, and Abin Nagara a carpenter (*nagar* = carpenter or joiner).

Their religious function was primarily to teach Bible and Jewish law. Depending on their capabilities, they could be elected *nasi*, president of the community, Av Beth Din, head of the religious court, or simply an arbiter on ritual and civil law. At all times they were exemplars of moral, ethical and charitable conduct.

These duties were carried out in an honorary capacity. The only payment received (in necessitous cases) was for eessential expenses incurred during that period in which public welfare work and education were being carried out (Talmud, Shabbat 114).

The respect accorded to rabbis was greater even than that shown to parents. The Talmud frequently emphasises the importance of study and the honour due to those who are wise: "The elder in knowledge is to be revered even more than the elder in years" (Kiddushin 32).

Today, the rabbi's role, besides being pastoral, has broadened to include educational and charitable work in the wider community. Such duties as visiting patients in hospitals emerged only in the last century and seem to have been confined to ministers serving communities in Britain and its colonies.

Many age-old duties have, of course, been retained. Sermons, for example, were delivered every Sabbath even in talmudic times (Sotah 41).

One commentator of the Shulchan Aruch (Ba'er Heitev, Orach Chaim 151) states that it is forbidden to sleep during a sermon since, besides being disrespectful towards the speaker, "one closes one's eyes to the words of

the Torah." In such cases, it is the duty of a neighbour to awaken the slumberer.

With the ever-widening range of the rabbi's responsibilities, it eventually became the custom to engage him on a full-time basis and for the congregation to pay him a salary. In some countries the State paid (and still pays) the salary, since the rabbi is the officially appointed leader of the Jewish community.

Strict guidelines have been set for rabbinical conduct. Isaiah Horowitz, one of the greatest rabbinical leaders of European Jewry, declared that a rabbi's mode of life should be beyond reproach and that he should endeavour to improve the Jewish masses religiously, morally and ethically (Sh'lah 1).

The chazan, or cantor, has the task of preserving the heritage of synagogue music. Throughout the generations, on each of the services — on Sabbaths, festivals, fast days, weddings or funerals — the *sheliach tzibbur* (emissary of the congregation) has faithfully adhered to the traditional mode (*nusach*) and has thereby set the mood of the occasion.

Originally, the chazan's duties included looking after the synagogue and its ancillary buildings, teaching the young, making announcements and attending to the welfare of the worshippers. During the Middle Ages his status was enhanced by being permanently engaged to conduct the services and to work alongside the rabbi in his communal activities.

Since the nineteenth century, cantorial training has included the study of music and courses in voice production and technique. But the essential qualifications for a competent chazan as laid down by Jewish law, are, as always, modesty, refinement and learning.

Not only is it necessary for the chazan to have a pleasant voice, but good pronunciation and enunciation are also important (Talmud, Megila 24). His training must include a study of the Bible and the Siddur, together with a sound knowledge of halacha.

Song and prayer have been a traditional combination in Jewish liturgy since Temple times (though undue prolongation of the service, says the "Avodat Yisrael," is considered an excessive burden on the congregation). Chazanut has its origins in the Levitical singing during Temple services.

The office of shamash (attendant or servant) came into vogue during the Middle Ages, when he was an official vested with considerable responsibility and power. The "Jewish Year Book" of 1897 states: "The shamash assessed the members of the congregation according to their means. He was a sort of permanent Under-Secretary of State, who governed while the *parnas* (warden or *gabbai*) was supposed to rule."

The modern shamash assists in the smooth running of the services by distributing prayer-books and apportioning the mitzvot. It is also customary for him to help in administrative duties, in making communal announcements and in undertaking the maintenance of the ritual objects.

The tasks and responsibilities are varied and valued, and one who is well-versed in Jewish learning can invariably assist in almost every facet of synagogue activity. The relationship of the shamash to the congregant has become that of a confidant and has reached the level of familiarity rather than of servility.

The Torah

THE WORD Torah is derived from the Hebrew *horah,* to teach or instruct, to show the way or point out. This has been the role of the Torah for thousands of years, with its natural concomitant of being the most sacred object in the synagogue.

The Torah is read on a regular basis four times a week, as decreed by the Lawgiver himself, Moses, who said that three days should not pass without a public reading of the Law (Maimonides, Hilchot Tefila 12).

Moses laid down that the number to be called up on a Sabbath was seven, and Ezra, together with the Men of the Great Assembly, ruled that on Mondays, Thursdays and Sabbath afternoons only three people were called up (Talmud, Baba Kama 82). The number prescribed by Ezra is strictly adhered to, though in some synagogues the number laid down by Moses for Shabbat-morning readings is supplemented by additional aliyot for special occasions.

The compulsory and regular recital of the Torah on three days of every week has enabled the wise and the humble alike to become familiar with the essence of Judaism, thus ensuring its position of honour as the central part of the synagogue service throughout the week.

The sefer Torah is, in a sense, the God-given constitution of the Jewish people, covering the entire spectrum of social and ethical behaviour. Its sacredness derives from traditional Judaism's belief in the spiritual-historical event which took place at Sinai and made manifest in the *Torah shebiktav,* the Written Law, one of the cornerstones of our faith.

In antiquity, all books were written in the form of a scroll. The High Priest in the Temple read from a scroll on Yom Kippur and so emphasised the centrality and sanctity of the sefer Torah. In consequence, the text must be written with utmost care, conforming in every detail to the requirements set down by the massoratic scholars who lived in Tiberias between the sixth and the ninth centuries and sealed by Aaron Ben-Asher in the first half of the tenth century.

These details include a system of accents and vocalisation, or cantillation, which are not, however, written into the scroll itself, since the text consists only of unvowelled characters.

The oldest source of Jewish music, biblical cantillation, is halachically required for the reading of the Scriptures (Talmud, Megila 32); anyone who recites them without the appropriate melody is deemed to show scant regard for the text and its meaning. The traditional tunes must be chanted, says the Talmud, for "whoever intones the Holy Scriptures in the manner of secular song abuses the Torah."

The *neginot,* musical signs, are unique in their notation, a form of musical shorthand, and although identical signs are used for all the books of the Bible, the notes vary considerably from section to section and from book to book. The *neginot* serve both as an interpretation of the text and as an aid to memory; the melody, said the rabbis, helps one to recall what has been studied (Shabbat 106).

The psalmist declared that the study of Torah through song brings joy: "The precepts of the Lord are right, rejoicing the heart" (Psalm 19). The Torah and its precepts are themselves compared to a song: ". . . now, therefore, write this song for yourself" (Deuteronomy 31), which is also interpreted as a positive commandment to write or possess a sefer Torah.

A person is permitted to write a scroll himself, to buy one or to have one written by a scribe on his behalf. Even one letter written or corrected by oneself is considered sufficient for fulfilling the mitzva to write an entire Torah scroll.

For this reason the custom has developed of filling in the outlines of letters prepared by a scribe for the first and last paragraphs of the scroll. This ceremony is known as *siyum ha-Torah,* the completion of the Torah scroll.

It is forbidden to sell a sefer Torah except for the purpose of providing the means necessary for marrying, for paying a ransom or for Jewish education. If a scroll accidentally falls to the ground, the whole congregation is obliged to fast for a day.

The hallmark of Israel's distinction and distinctiveness is reflected in the way its written word has remained inviolate throughout the generations. The Midrash illustrates this by stating that, when Moses said to the Children of Israel, "Both those who are with us today and those who are not with us today" (Deuteronomy 29), he did not say "standing" with us today, but simply "with us today."

The souls of unborn beings were also present at Sinai. Even those who were to arise in future generation received their inspiration from Sinai (Shemot Rabbah 28).

Reading of the Law and the Haftara

AS OBSERVED previously, the reading of the Law, *kriat hatorah,* takes place at least four times a week — on Shabbat mornings and afternoons and on Monday and Thursday mornings, provided, of course, that a minyan is present.

The Torah itself contains no specific reference to this procedure, but a midrashic hint as to its derivation is found in the words, "And they went three days in the wilderness and found no water" (Exodus 15).

The sages compared water, man's lifeblood, to the Torah, the essential nourishment in the life of the Jew. Since the Children of Israel became weary and quarrelsome after three days' lack of water, the inference was drawn that they could not be deprived of spiritual "water" for longer than that period.

Explaining why Mondays and Thursdays were chosen as regular days for the Torah readings, the Talmud states that these were busy market-days when people gathered in large numbers in one central area. Moreover, Moses ascended Mount Sinai on a Thursday to receive the Torah and descended on a Monday, so that these days were considered as special days of mercy and favour (Baba Kamma 82). The Sabbath was the only other day that could be included in the three-day-cycle calculation.

Originally, the king, priest or prophet read the whole of the weekly portion, the *sidra,* to the congregation. Later, the portion was divided into seven sections *(parshiyot),* each being read by a different person.

In time, with a deterioration in the standard of learning among the laity, it was decided to revert to the original procedure and to appoint a special officiant, a *ba'al koreh* or *ba'al keriah,* to read the sidra, out of consideration for those who might not be able to read it themselves.

The number of people called up to receive an *aliya* (lit, "ascent") to the reading of the Law varies according to the particular service. On Mondays, Thursdays and Shabbat afternoons it is three; during *chol hamoed* (the intermediate days of festivals) and on New Moons, four; on festivals, five; on Yom Kippur, six; and on Sabbath mornings, seven.

The first to be called up is always a Cohen (providing, of course, that one is present), and not even the President of Israel, were he to be in synagogue, could claim any preference. Next comes a Levite and thereafter Israelites.

There is an order of precedence for those who have suffered a bereavement, are observing a yahrzeit, or celebrating a birth or an anniversary. It was the Maharal of Prague, Rabbi Yehuda Loew ben Bezalel (1512-1609), who formulated the order of *aliyot* as we know it today.

When called up to the Torah, it is customary for one to approach the bima by the quickest route, showing eagerness to hear the Torah reading; on returning to one's seat, however, one should take the longest route, displaying a reluctance to leave the scroll.

Once the Torah reading is finished, the scroll is lifted up, *hagba'ha,* and rolled together, *gelila.* Many would be surprised to learn that the Talmud considers the last mitzva to be the greatest honour of all those connected with *kriat hatorah* (Megila 32).

Where, for one reason or another, no complete or kosher sefer Torah is available for public reading, it is permitted to use an incomplete scroll or a printed Chumash in order that the reading of the Law is not neglected. No blessing, however, may be recited before or after the reading in these circumstances (Aruch Hashulchan 143).

On Sabbaths, festivals and fast days, *kriat hatorah* is followed by the reading of a passage from one of the books of the Prophets. This section is called the haftara — "taking one's leave," or "completion."

The theme of the haftara is invariably linked with a similar subject in that day's Torah reading. The portion of the Torah, for example, dealing with the twelve spies sent by Moses (in the weekly sidra of Shelach) has as its haftara a comparable incident decades later when Joshua was in command of the Israelites.

The custom of reading a portion from the Prophets evolved at a time when, under foreign domination (before the Hasmonean revolt), Jews were forbidden to read the Torah in public. The prophetical portion which contained a similar theme was read in its place.

At least 21 verses were read from the Prophets to enable each person to hear the three verses which would have been read to him had he been called up to the Torah. Although the decree was later revoked, the custom of reading the haftara was retained.

Talmudic literature refers to specific haftarot connected with the festivals and special Sabbaths. In these cases the prophetical reading deals with the particular occasion in the Jewish calender and is not linked to the reading of the Law. The haftarot for ordinary Sabbaths were fixed after the talmudic period, in the sixth century.

The person honoured with the reading of the haftara is called the *maftir,* "one who concludes." He is called up to hear the repetition of the last few verses of the sidra. Thereafter, he recites the haftara (to a special melody) either from a printed text or from a parchment scroll, preceded and followed by prayers of thanksgiving and gratitude.

The Siddur

IF ONE WANTS to gain an insight into the history of the Jewish people, the siddur is as good a place as any to make a start. It illustrates the development of Israel's relationship with God, while at the same time giving ethical guidance and placing strong emphasis on man's duties and priorities.

The word siddur derives from *seder*, "order," since the sequence of the prayer-book coincides with the frequency with which the prayers are recited during the yearly cycle of events: the daily service, the Sabbath and the festivals, the milestones of marriage, birth, barmitzvah and death, the living experiences of the Jew on every level and at all times.

Early Jewish tradition prohibited the writing of the Torah and the prayers on the ground that, in order to keep Judaism alive, it was essential to memorise the texts. With the increasing dispersion of the Jews, however, the preservation of that tradition was placed in jeopardy and the rabbis permitted the Oral Law to be written down.

This ruling was based on the verse in Psalm 119, "It is time for the Lord to work; they have made void Thy law." Action had to be taken to prevent a general transgression of the Torah. Thus, the Bible, siddur, Mishna and Talmud became the literary classics of the Jewish people.

The prayers in the siddur were, in the main, to be in Hebrew, the holy tongue *(leshon hakodesh)*. Israel's historical language gave a sense of solemnity to the service while also illustrating the unity of the Jewish people. Such sections of the community as the Hellenistic Jews, who felt that they could dispense with Hebrew in their worship, disappeared from the Jewish scene and became totally assimilated.

The forerunner of the prayer book was a collection of 100 blessings formulated in talmudic times by Rabbi Meir, who ruled that everyone was obliged to recite that number of blessings each day. These are retained in the siddur, as are those blessings in the grace after meals whose authorship is traditionally ascribed to Moses, Joshua and Solomon.

In the ninth century, the first

collection of prayers for a siddur was produced by Rabbi Amram Gaon at the request of the Jews of Spain. Each section included a summary of the relevant religious laws (*halachot*), as well as additional blessings and prayers for special occasions.

This was followed by the prayer-book of the greatest scholar of Babylonian Jewry, the tenth-century Saadiah Gaon (which is in print under the title "Siddur Rav Saadiah Gaon"), and then by the "Machzor Vitry" of Rabbi Simcha ben Shmuel, a pupil of the commentator Rashi.

The term "machzor," employed here to indicate the prayers in the daily and yearly "circle," came in the course of time to be used exclusively for the festival prayer-book; siddur, an abbreviation of *seder tefilot* (order of prayers) referred in the main to the daily prayer-book.

With the invention of printing in the fifteenth century came many editions of the siddur. The Sephardi rite took on a form of its own in the sixteenth century, with the prayers laid down by the cabalist rabbi, Isaac Luria of Safed, the Ari.

Among the most popular modern editions of the siddur are the version of the Rev Simeon Singer, commonly known as the "Singer's Prayer Book," and the companion volumes published by Israel Abrahams and later by Chief Rabbi Joseph Hertz.

These translated editions were designed to assist the worshipper in his understanding of the prayers and not to replace the original text of the prayer-book.

Besides creating a unifying bond among Jews the world over in times of distress and dispersion, the siddur also played an important role in fulfilling the dream of the re-establishment of a Jewish homeland in the Holy Land. Indeed, says the Talmud, some of the prayers mentioning Eretz Yisrael predate the Children of Israel's entry into the Promised Land, over 3,500 years ago.

Nor do the prayers for the restoration of Zion and the ingathering of the exiles speak only of Israel's welfare; they call, too, for the spiritual enlightenment and moral growth of all mankind. The siddur is, in fact, replete with prayers for universal justice, understanding and righteousness, for morality and, above all, for universal peace.

The siddur has been called "the mirror and soul of the Jewish people." Its pages reflect the yearnings and doctrines of our people, their intellectual and spiritual riches, psalms, affirmations of faith, messages of hope, and Torah teachings. The whole gamut of Jewish belief is gathered between its covers. history and belief is gathered between its covers.

The Machzor. Prayer

THE PRAYER-BOOK used for the five main festivals mentioned in the Torah — Rosh Hashana, Yom Kippur, Succot, Pesach and Shavuot — is known as the *machzor*, "cycle," the term originally used for the daily prayer-book, the siddur.

In the course of time, the prayers recited during the year became too numerous, and the volume too bulky, for the machzor to be published as a single unit. The synagogue liturgy became prolix in style and a sixteenth-century publisher took the initiative of issuing two separate publications, one containing the regular weekday and Shabbat prayers and the other for use during the *shalosh regalim*, the three pilgrim festivals, and the *yamim noraim*, the High Holy-days.

The machzor, with its added liturgical poetry and hymns (*piyyutim*), was later itself subdivided into separate volumes for Pesach, Shavuot and Succot, and for Rosh Hashana and Yom Kippur.

At first, the pioneer printers followed the forms of prayer of the local community and produced only that number of machzorim required in each area. But this was clearly not a viable proposition as far as the publishing business was concerned, and in due course far larger quantities were printed for use by Jewish communities not only nationally, but throughout the world.

The main communities, each with their own customs, and often variants of prayer, were the Ashkenazim, Sephardim, Chasidim and Yemenites. Their rites and traditions were incorporated into their respective machzorim.

The *minhagim* (customs) peculiar to each community often disappeared as the printing processes became ever more complex. But the Frankfurt Jews, for example, whose descendants are scattered over the globe, have continued to form their own congregations and have held on with tenacity to their original customs and traditions.

The sages who formulated the prayers in the siddur and machzor weighed every word before agreeing to its entry into the sacred volumes. "He who changes the text of our authoritatively ordained prayers does not fulfil his obligations in praying," said the Talmud (Berachot 40).

Every word and every paragraph has the force of history and tradition behind it. Each has been selected to induce *kavana*, devotion and intention, the chief prerequisites of prayer.

"One should not pray in a mechanical way, like the chattering of a raven or a parrot, but each word should be uttered thoughtfully and with full intent," says the "Kuzari" of Yehuda Halevi. "Communal prayer has many advantages. Its blessing rests on everyone, each receiving his or her portion."

The language of the prayer books, gleaned from the Bible and from the works of our greatest poets, expresses profound thoughts on human life and aspirations. An authority on the psychology and history of prayer has written: "Formularies of prayer can kindle, strengthen and purify religious life. Even in prayers recited without complete understanding, the worshipper is conscious that he has to do with something holy, that the words which he uses bring him into relation with God. In spite of all externalism, prescribed prayer has acted at all times as a mighty level in spiritual life."

The Hebrew word for prayer, *tefila*, is derived from *hitpallel*, to examine or judge oneself. The English word implies entreating the Almighty, from the Latin *precaria*, to beg (similar to the German *gebet*). Judaism thus teaches that prayer is a means of reaching greater heights, a way of judging oneself in the light of lofty truths and ideals.

The codes of Jewish law stress that in all acts of worship the fundamental requirement is sincerity. The prophet Isaiah condemns routine, mechanical and meaningless repetition of services. And the Talmud consistently emphasises the importance of being in the right frame of mind before and during prayer.

"The pious old men of yore used to wait for an hour before praying, so that they might concentrate their thoughts on the Father in Heaven" (Berachot 5). "One should not recite one's prayers as if reading a letter."

It is forbidden to raise one's voice in prayer, although the words must be distinctly pronounced (and heard by oneself) and should constitute a "service of the heart."

To benefit from prayer, the Jew must know how, when and what to pray. Moses was the exemplar in this respect. Asking for forgiveness for the sin of the Golden Calf, he prayed for forty days and forty nights; yet when he pleaded for his sister's recovery from leprosy, he used only five short words — "O Lord, do heal her." In both instances they were answered.

The amida and the kaddish conclude with the words *oseh shalom bimromav*, "May he who makes peace in Heaven make peace on earth," at which point the worshipper takes three steps backwards. A Chasidic thought has it that if peace is to be made, then standing obstinately in one place will not help. Sometimes one should be prepared to step backwards, to make concessions, in the cause of peace.

Special Prayers and Blessings

SPECIAL BLESSINGS and prayers are recited on very many occasions throughout the year, particularly on those days when the reading of the Law takes place. They are all in keeping with the talmudical statement, derived from Psalm 24, that mankind may enjoy the fullness of the earth, which belongs to God, after consecrating it with benedictions.

While the Torah is out of the ark, it became customary during the gaonic period to include pleas for recovery from illness or for the granting of blessings of health and happiness to members of one's family. These came under the heading of *mi sheberach*, "He who blesses" — the first words of the prayers being offered up.

The blessing is invoked on the person called up to the Torah and usually includes an offering for charitable purposes. A general *mi sheberach*, also dating back to gaonic times, is recited every Sabbath for those who work for the good of the community or contribute in one way or another towards the synagogue and its activities.

A prayer of gratitude on recovery from severe illness, avoidance of great danger or survival from a perilous voyage, known as *birkat hagomel*, is recited after the second of the two blessings on the Torah. It is mentioned in the Talmud (Berachot 54) and is suggested in Psalm 107. Also known by its Yiddish name, *gomel benschen*, it elicits a response from the congregation that the Almighty may continue to deal kindly with the one who offers up the prayer.

Another prayer referred to by its opening words is the memorial prayer, *el malei rachamim*, which originated in talmudic times and is recited at funeral services and on yahrzeits, as well as on other occasions of remembrance.

The onset of the new moon (with the exception of Tishri) is heralded on the preceding Sabbath morning. Known as *m'vorechin hachodesh* (blessing the month), the prayer is recited before the public pronouncement of the name and day of the month, commemorating the proclamation made by the Beth Din in ancient times. Since the witnesses who

reported the appearance of the new moon were required to stand while giving their evidence, so must the congregation stand throughout the ceremony (Orach Chayim 417).

The prayer before the declaration is derived from the Talmud (Berachot 16) and was uttered daily, with the omission of certain words, by the founder of the Babylonian Academy of Sura, Abba Areka (Rav), who died in 247 CE. Sephardim do not recite this prayer, but commence directly with the announcement of the new month.

The open-air ceremony of *kiddush halevana*, sanctification of the new moon, takes place between the fourth and the fourteenth of the month, when the moon is visible. Psalms and prayers are recited based on talmudic formulae (Sanhedrin 42) which link the moon's reappearance to the

spiritual renewal of the Jew and the constant rebirth of His people.

A meditational prayer in Aramaic, recited just before the Torah is taken out of the ark, is *b'rich shemei*, "blessed be the name"; this is derived from the mystical cabalistic work, the Zohar ("Brightness"), attributed to the second-century Rabbi Shimon ben Yochai.

The Zohar introduces this inspiring prayer with the words: "When the Torah is taken out in the assembly to be read before the congregation, the heavenly gates of mercy are opened and the divine love awakens. It is then fitting to recite:

Blessed be the name . . . Not in man do I put my trust, nor do I rely on any angel, but only in the God of heaven who is the God of truth, whose Torah is truth and whose prophets are truth. In Him I put my trust, to His holy and glorious name I utter praises. May it be Thy will to open my heart to Thy Law . . . and of the hearts of all Thy people Israel for good, for life and for peace.

The best-known of all the prayers is the *kaddish*, written in Aramaic and appearing in five different forms in the siddur. Associated mainly with mourning, it is, however, a prayer which sanctifies and glorifies God's name, calling for the redemption of mankind and for "peace and life."

The prayer was originally recited in talmudic times by a teacher or preacher at the conclusion of his lecture or sermon. Today it marks the end of sections of the service; the earliest allusion to its recitation by mourners is in the Machzor Vitri of 1208.

The essential part of the kaddish consists of the congregational response: "Let His great name be blessed for ever and ever and to all eternity," similar to the declaration of Daniel (2:20). It binds together generations in love and respect, making the hearts of parents and children beat in eternal unison.

The prayer for the welfare of the State of Israel was composed in 1948, soon after the re-establishment of the Jewish State following 2,000 years of exile. It calls for peace not only in Eretz Israel, but "over all the dwellers on earth."

The Sofer

POSSIBLY the oldest communal profession in Judaism is that of the scribe *(sofer)*. The title is found in the Bible (II Samuel 8; II Kings 19; Ezra 4) and his task, initially, was to interpret the Torah to the people.

When the Jews returned from Babylon, there was a demand for men who could instruct the masses and give them a better understanding of the Law of Moses. Some commentators, such as the Targum Jonathan, in fact refer to Moses and Aaron as "*sofrim* of Israel."

One of the best known of the scribes was Ezra, who was largely responsible for the spiritual revival of his time and who became known as Ezra Ha'Sofer, described in the book carrying his name as "a ready scribe in the Law of Moses." During his time the scribes were engaged in elevating Judaism to a higher intellectual plane through the revival of Hebrew, which had been neglected during the Babylonian exile, and in designing a suitable and graceful script.

Later, two kinds of professional scribes emerged. One was known as *sofer s'tam*, encompassing the words "*sefer Torah*," "*tefilin*" and "*mezuza*"; he was engaged in writing the principal religious appurtenances of the community.

The other was called *sofer ha'kahal* and acted as the recording clerk of the Beth Din; it was he who prepared bills of divorce *(gittin)* and who worked as communal public notary. Today's sofer acts in both capacities.

The scribe was considered an essential part of the Jewish community. In fact, the Talmud declared that an educated person was not to live in a town in which a sofer did not reside (Sanhedrin 17).

It is recorded that the scribe was so indispensable that people were cautioned not to allow him to become too rich, thereby reducing his need to write for a livelihood. In the event, the Talmud reveals that scribes were not blessed with riches (Pesachim 50).

The sofer is expected to undergo a rigorous period of training, with a host of complicated regulations. Great care has to be paid to spelling, and any omission or mistake renders his output *pasul*, unfit for the purposes of fulfilling the commandment.

The scribe must be a pious and learned Jew of exemplary character, and all his writings must be *lishma*, for the sacred purpose for which the item is to be used. He is required to write a sefer Torah by copying the text from a model guide *(tikkun)* prepared by an expert, and not to rely on memory; "Let your eyes look right on, and let your eyelids look straight in front of you" (Proverbs 4).

Certain letters in the Torah are "crowned" with *taggin*, three prongs or strokes, while others are dotted above. The correct spacing of the Torah passages *(parashiyot)* must be carefully adhered to, and the spaces between each letter and word must comply with traditional regulations.

Many letters differ from the printed versions and only an experienced scribe is able to write them correctly. The Talmud devotes a whole tractate, Sofrim, to the work and duties of the traditional scribe, with the sages remarking that the "competitive spirit among scribes or scholars increases wisdom" (Baba Batra 21). The term *kinat sofrim* is a modern idiom for "academic rivalry."

The materials used for the sefer Torah, tefilin and mezuza include parchment produced from a kosher animal, durable black ink prepared from a formula known only to experts, and a quill pen.

A stylus and ruler are used to mark 43 imperceptible lines on the parchment, so that the sofer can write in straight lines and with equally spaced letters and words. The text is written in columns about five inches wide, allowing *l'mishpechoteichem* (Exodus 12:21)—the longest word in the Torah—to be written three times in one line.

The sefer Torah is written in a square script known as *k'tav ashuri*; Ashkenazim use a type of script described in the Talmud, while Sephardim employ a version similar to the printed letters of the Hebrew alphabet.

Two sections of the Torah are written differently from the rest: one is the Song of the Sea (or Song of Moses), *shirat hayam* (Exodus 15), which the Israelites chanted after

crossing the Red Sea. The other is *shirat ha'azinu*, Moses' final farewell speech: "Give ear, ye heavens, and I will speak; and let the earth hear the words of my mouth . . ." (Deuteronomy 32).

The first song is spaced out to resemble interlocking bricks in a wall, symbolic of the walls of water into which God divided the sea; the other is written in prose format, but with a space down the centre of the column of script.

In the course of time, the work of the scribe was elevated to that of the artist and the scribes of Alexandria were especially renowned for their skill in illumination. The talent of the sofer can best be seen in the work of an illuminated scroll of Esther, where it is permissible to draw around the columns of the text.

The marriage document, the *ketuba*, also lends itself to appropriate ornamental designs, framing the formula read out during the wedding ceremony. Decorative *ketubot* are often displayed in the homes of newly married couples.

In writing a mezuza or tefilin, the sofer observes the same rules as those for a sefer Torah, except that the words may be written from memory since, comparatively few in number, they are more familiar to him (Talmud, Megila 18). Most scribes, however, still prefer to copy from a text.

The Gabbai, Board/Council. The Congregation

THE TITLE *parnas,* president or warden of a congregation, was formerly accorded to the religious leader and administrator of a community. The Talmud asks: "Who is a scholar worthy of being appointed as parnas of the congregation? He who is asked about a law from any source ... and is able to answer it" (Shabbat 114).

The Jerusalem Talmud records the appointment of prominent scholars, such as Rabbi Akiva, as parnasim of the congregation, while elsewhere it speaks of Moses, Aaron and Miriam as being the ideal type of person to act as parnas since they demonstrated the qualities of leadership and were able to mix easily with people.

Early on, the parnas — the word derives from a root meaning "to provide" or "to support" — was responsible for the distribution of alms to the poor. In the Middle Ages he became lay leader, or president, of the congregation, having been elected by the rank-and-file membership.

From the earliest times, raised seats were allocated in the synagogue to those holding this honoured position. They were placed either on, to the side or in front of the bima, but always facing the congregation, so that every worshipper could be seen by the parnasim (Talmud, Succot 51). This was necessary for the allocation of mitzvot.

Around the sixteenth century, the sole responsibility of teaching and making halachic decisions devolved on to the rabbi, and the administrative duties of the congregation were handled by the parnas. The lay leader also came to be known as the *gabbai* (treasurer), since the collector of taxes and levies was originally known as the *gabbai tzedaka.*

Today these are honorary positions; the parnas is generally known as the warden, and the gabbai as the financial representative. The Sephardim use the term *parnas presidente* to denote the lay leader of the congregation.

The method of election or appointment depended to a great extent on local custom. Some early congregations had written regulations called *takkanot* — similar to the

printed bye-laws of the present-day United Synagogue of London — but when many of them drafted their own constitutions in the vernacular, the Hebrew titles were discarded by the wayside.

Parnasim presided over elected bodies of synagogue policy-makers variously known as boards of management, councils or committees. Today it is these bodies which hold the purse-strings, appoint the religious leaders and officials and administer the various charitable and welfare activities of the community.

Many synagogue members aspire to become parnas or gabbai. Perhaps they are encouraged by the saying in the Talmud (Yoma 22), "As soon as a man is appointed an administrator (parnas) of a community, he becomes rich"!

A minimum of ten male worshippers above the age of 13 is required to form a *minyan,* a congregational quorum. They are then entitled to merit the official designation of a holy congregation, *kehila kedosha,* which is considered to be sanctified by the Divine Presence.

Among the reasons given for the number ten is that in the story of the ten spies sent by Moses to report on the Holy Land, the word for a congregation, *eidah,* appears (Numbers 15). Earlier, Abraham, urged God to save Sodom if ten righteous men were to be found there (Genesis 18); and later, Boaz gathered round him ten elders of the city in order to make a statement regarding Naomi (Ruth 4).

A minyan is necessary for all public worship that falls under the heading *tefila betzibur* — such as the repetition of the amida, the reading of the Law and the recitation of kaddish. "Nine rabbis," says an old Yiddish maxim, "cannot make a minyan, but ten shoemakers can."

The concept of minyan men was once maintained by the "ten idlers," *asara batlanim,* who were kept by the congregation solely to ensure that religious life, even in the smallest community, was guaranteed by the existence of a congregational quorum. Public worship emphasises the Jewish doctrine of social responsibility; it is the spiritual link that unites one Jew to another and, through them all, to *K'lal Yisrael* — the community of Israel — and to God.

Although Judaism recognises the genuine spiritual value of private devotion and prayer, congregational services are regarded as being more uplifting and inspiring and more conducive to *d'veikut,* attachment to, and communion with, God.

In order to function as a compact community *(kehila),* Jewish life needs a cohesive force catering for the needs and welfare of its adherents. The most highly developed *kehila* was that formed in sixteenth-century Poland, where four provinces amalgamated to form a supreme Council of Four Lands.

The council served as a judicial body, established schools and yeshivot and enforced Jewish law and ethics, as well as the law of the State. This created unity of thought and action, affording an opportunity for the application of Jewish law in everyday life.

In all these activities the synagogue remained the central power-house of the community, whether as *bet haknesset,* house of assembly, *bet hatefila,* house of prayer, or *bet hamidrash,* house of learning. It served the spiritual and social needs of the Jew and to this day embraces its original functions as a place for assembly, prayer and study.

Names of sections of the services. Nusach

THE FIRST divine worship of the day is, naturally enough, the morning service, shacharit, recited before the normal daily routine begins. With the exception of Rosh Hashana and Yom Kippur, it is the longest of the three services and consists of five distinctive sections.

These commence with the morning blessings, *birkot hashachar*, originally recited privately as each act — washing, dressing, and so on — was performed. Later, these blessings of thanksgiving were incorporated into the main body of the service.

Anyone who prays daily additionally fulfils one of the mitzvot required of every Jew — that of daily Torah study. The morning blessings include the Torah benediction, the priestly benediction (Numbers 6) and a mishna (Peah 81), ensuring that the worshipper has recited at least two pieces of study at the very start of the day. During this part of the service one may proceed at one's own pace, without the leadership of a chazan.

The morning service continues with a collection of psalms of thanksgiving, together with biblical verses of praise which conclude with Moses' song sung at the shore of the Red Sea. This section of the service, called *pesukei d'zimra* (passages of song), is expanded on Shabbat and the festivals to include nine additional psalms which speak of God's role in Israel's history, the paradox of man's frailty and his enormous potential, and the recognition of the Almighty's hand in nature.

The entire section is a kind of prologue to the formal part of the service, although it is considered public prayer and requires a *sheliach tzibbur*, leader of the congregation, to conduct the service. Ending on the exultant note of the Song of Moses (recited in a standing position), it passes from the informal to the main part of the shacharit service, which needs the presence of a minyan.

At the heart of the third section is the *shema*, the first paragraph of which is written in the singular as a call both to the individual Jew and to the Jewish people as a composite unit. The ensuing two paragraphs deal with some of the fundamental principles of

"And you shall talk of them [My commandments] . . . when you lie down and when you rise up" — from the first paragraph of the shema

Judaism and the commandment regarding the wearing of tzitzit.

The fourth section of the morning service is known as the *amida*, the "standing prayer," preceded by a plea for the redemption of Israel.

This, said the sages, is the highest aspiration of the Jew and the Talmud rules that the prayer for redemption should be followed immediately by the *amida* without even an interruption for the response of *amen* at the end of the blessing which precedes it (*ga'al yisrael*). For this reason, the chazan recites the words in a whisper, inaudible to the congregation.

Shacharit draws to a close with the traditional *aleinu*, which sings the praises of God as King and Ruler of the universe. To enable him to leave the synagogue remembering the ancient Temple service, the worshipper concludes with the psalm of the day, *shir shel yom*, retaining the levitical custom of reciting a psalm for each of the seven days of the week.

The afternoon service, mincha, is the shortest of the three daily services. On Sabbath afternoons it includes a brief reading from the Law — the opening passage of the following week's sidra.

Emphasising the importance of the afternoon service, Rabbi Jacob ben Asher, author of the "Tur," stated

that while the morning service preceded the day's work and the evening service followed it, mincha was recited while one was still occupied with work and it thus required a special effort to stop for prayer (Orach Chayim, 232). The time for the mincha service is also considered the "hour of mercy" since Elijah's prayer at Mount Carmel found acceptance at that time of the day (I Kings 18).

Finally, maariv is recited as the day draws to a close, when we renew our plea for God's protection and solicitude. The *shema* is again recited, according to the injunction *b'shochbecha uvekumecha*, "when you lie down and when you rise up" (Deuteronomy 6). Some congregations have an interval between mincha and maariv to allow for a period of study.

Two further services are not recited daily — musaf, the additional service, which is said on Sabbaths, New Moons and festivals, and neila, the concluding prayer on Yom Kippur. Musaf includes a special amida after the Torah reading and refers to the appropriate day during one of the seven blessings which it contains.

Neila is regarded as the most important of the Yom Kippur services and many worshippers remain standing throughout it. Its climax is reached with the congregational proclamation of the *shema*, followed by the doxology used in the Temple, *baruch shem* . . .(blessed be the Name) and concluding with Elijah's declaration at Mount Carmel, "The Lord, He is God" (I Kings 18:39).

Each of the five services and their incorporated sections has its own unique chants, transmitted from generation to generation; even a layman who leads the service must be familiar with the *nusach* (prayer mode), otherwise, say the rabbis, the congregation will not benefit from the purpose of public worship.

Synagogue melody is regarded as one of the threefold pillars which maintain the link between the Creator and the people of Israel: through song and melody the Jew has constantly been able to renew himself in the service of the synagogue.

Concluding Hymns

IN TEMPLE times, instrumental music played an important role in religious services. In Solomon's Temple there were twenty-four conductors, who were assistants to the three chief conductors for the 288 singer-musicians, as recorded in the First Book of Chronicles.

Today, music is almost totally absent from the synagogue. Various reasons have been advanced for the exclusion of instrumental and orchestral music from our services, the main one being that rabbinic law prohibited the playing of an instrument on the Sabbaths and festivals outside the Temple (Eruvin 104).

After the destruction of the Temples, the absence of instrumental music in the synagogue served as yet another sign of mourning for the loss of Jewry's glorious past, strengthening our longing for its restoration. And when the non-Jewish world followed the Jewish initiative of holding services accompanied by choirs and organ, the principle of *chukat hagoy*, of not imitating Gentile practices (Leviticus 18), also became involved.

In pre-Second World War European communities it was customary to permit orchestral music in the synagogue on Chanucah and Purim, so that these minor festivals would take on a joyous — even jolly — atmosphere. The marriage service has always been allowed musical accompaniment in order to enhance the event.

With the absence of instrumental music in most of our services, the place of *nusach*, mode of prayer, takes on a special significance. Its main function is to assist in the concentration, spirit and devotion of the worshipper in every prayer he recites or hears.

The eminent fourteenth-century scholar, Rabbi Jacob Molin (known as the Maharil), was in the forefront of the ruling that the traditional melodies, universally adopted, should not be changed. This insistence on *nusach* is largely responsible for the preservation of unity in the musical tradition of the synagogue services.

Rabbi Molin's ruling was, however, restricted to the established sections

of the Sabbath, festival and weekday services. Improvisation, or the introduction of special musical settings, was allowed for other parts of the service, such as *ein keloheinu, anim zemirot* and *adon olam,* where the composer is free to beautify the service in his own way, and to encourage congregational singing.

Ein keloheinu is recited by Sephardi and Chasidic congregations at the end of every morning service (weekdays included), while Ashkenazi communities in the diaspora sing it only on Sabbaths and festivals; in Israel, however, the Ashkenazim, too, recite it daily.

Rashi pointed out that the initial letters of the first three lines and the first words of the last two lines form the words *amen baruch ata,* "Amen, blessed art Thou."

It is interesting to note that *ein keloheinu* opens with a statement and carries on with a question. This has been interpreted to mean that in Judaism one must first have conviction and belief and only then put forward philosophical questions.

Ein keloheinu is followed by a passage from the Talmud (Keritot 6), thus ending the service as it began — with the recitation of a talmudic passage. The hymn was mentioned in the siddur compiled by Amram Gaon and Maimonides as early as the twelfth century.

The lines of another hymn usually sung towards the end of the service, *anim zemirot,* are chanted alternately by chazan and congregation. Its authorship has been attributed to Judah Hechasid (Judah the Saint), the thirteenth-century poet, philosopher

and mystic, of Regensburg, who was considered to have been the ideal Jew on account of his piety and learning.

The poetic beauty and emotional power of his work earned it the title of *shir hakavod,* "Hymn of Glory." Its importance is demonstrated by the fact that the congregation recites it standing before an open ark and that it is one of the concluding hymns sung on Kol Nidre night.

Many congregations have the custom of allowing a child to lead the recitation of *anim zemirot,* thereby encouraging youngsters to take a role in congregational worship. Numerous melodies have been composed for this awe-inspiring hymn.

The final hymn in services on Sabbaths, festivals and Kol Nidre night is *adon olam,* "Lord of the Universe." The authorship is unknown, some believing it to be one or other of the sages in the Persian diaspora during the Middle Ages, others attributing it to Solomon ibn Gabirol, who lived in Spain in the eleventh century.

Adon olam has become the unofficial anthem of the Jewish people. Almost every public function, sad or joyous, includes the singing of this beautiful hymn, which recounts the essence and greatness of God, His eternity, uniqueness, infinity and majesty.

Everyone, says the hymn, is sustained by God in times of trouble and it is through His protection and guidance that, awake or asleep, we entrust our body and spirit to Him. "To his hand I commend my spirit, when I sleep and when I wake. And with my spirit, my body also. God is with me; and I shall not be afraid."

The hymn has a universal appeal through its simplicity of language and religious belief. Many Jews are taught to recite *adon olam* every night before retiring to rest, falling asleep calmed by the pure and simple words of faith.

The three hymns mentioned here have given composers of synagogue music a unique opportunity to use their talents for the beautification of the service. In this they follow the example of King David and the prophet Samuel, who were among the first to establish the concept and art of music and song in worship.

'Derech Eretz' — Behaviour

CERTAIN Hebrew expressions from the Bible and Talmud have gained such currency over the centuries that the Jew has never been allowed to forget his obligations and responsibilities in his dealings with others.

These were terms rooted in the religious tradition of the Jewish people and, although a person may have removed himself far from synagogue life, he could not but express himself in the terminology which derived from the very source of Judaism. One word or phrase could encompass a whole idea — a concept, commandment or commentary — which in other philosophies would take pages to write.

A few examples in the next series of articles will demonstrate the value of these principles and their importance in day-to-day activities when meeting and dealing with people — whether in thought, speech or deed.

The rabbis in the Midrash (Vayikra 9) claimed that *derech eretz kodma la' Torah*, the correct behaviour of a person towards his fellow man preceded the giving of the Torah. The Talmud elucidates this by saying: "Without the Torah, we could have learned modesty from the cat, honesty from the ant, purity from the dove, and good manners from the rooster" (Eruvin 100).

It needed the Torah and its mitzvot, however, to teach one real *derech eretz* — the way of the world — for although it was possible to acquire good behaviour by following the example of animals, one could equally pick up the vice of cruelty which should not be imitated by man. As the Ethics of the Fathers put it: "Where there is no Torah, there can be no proper conduct, there can be no [life of the] Torah" (Avot 3).

Etiquette and dignified conduct are forever stressed in the pages of the Torah and the Talmud. When, for example, one speaks to a person, it is courteous first to address him by his name, as God called "Moses, Moses" before speaking to him (Exodus 3).

Women should be addressed before men, as (according to the Midrash) Moses did when he told the Children

of Israel to be prepared to receive the Torah at Sinai (Exodus 19). Such behaviour in public, said the rabbis, was designed to mirror the dignity and integrity of beings created in the image of God.

The term *derech eretz* is also used to describe respect for parents, teachers and elders. The Talmud (Sanhedrin 100) states that parents and teachers should not be called by their first names and that one should rise before "the hoary head," as commanded by the Torah (Leviticus 19:32).

The Midrash (Bamidbar 15) declares that one should honour an elderly person by not standing in his place or sitting in his seat, and by not contradicting his words. Maimonides adds (Talmud Torah 6) that any old person — Jew or non-Jew — should be accorded honour and a helping hand in accordance with the verse in Leviticus.

In his classical work, "Shaarei Teshuva," Rabbenu Jonah of Gerona stressed the honour and respect due to Torah scholars, particularly when speaking about them, whether in their presence or not.

The Mishna, in Avot 5, states that a wise and well-mannered person does not speak before being spoken to by one who is wiser than he; does not interrupt when another person is speaking; does not reply hastily; questions according to the subject and answers to the point; speaks about first things first and last things last; admits that which he does not understand; and acknowledges the truth.

Derech eretz has another meaning — one who is engaged in a trade, profession or occupation as a means of earning a livelihood, in other words, "practical living," as expressed in Avot (2:2).

Rabbi Gamliel is quoted in that Mishna as saying: "An excellent thing is the study of the Torah combined with some worldly occupation." Here the Hebrew for "wordly occupation" is *derech eretz*, the theory that principles must go hand-in-hand with practice, that a knowledge of the Torah must accompany the knowledge of a trade.

This ideal was espoused by the outstanding European thinker, Rabbi Samson Raphael Hirsch (1808-1888), whose *Torah im derech eretz* principle was formulated when he wrote: "The science of Torah and its emanating knowledge shall be for us the most important factor, an absolute and permanent axiom.

"All secular knowledge shall only be an auxiliary force designed to further the study and understanding of Torah; but it must always be *tofel* (subordinate) and Torah must remain the *ikkar* (principle or core)."

Another Torah scholar and spiritual leader, Rabbi Isaiah Horowitz (known as the Shela), who died in Tiberias in 1626, defined one who practised *derech eretz* as "a person who has upright conduct, deep humility and the possession of moral and ethical qualities which reflect themselves in being loved by God and man; being a man of peace who helps to preserve the world in both heavenly and mundane matters."

Since *derech eretz* is closely associated with the Torah itself, the Jew is enjoined to observe a code of behaviour which goes beyond the norm. It is regarded as an obligation of a religious nature, concerned primarily with decent and respectful conduct towards all mankind.

Justice/False Witness/Beth Din

NOBILITY of character presupposes a sense of fairness, integrity and justice. The Hebrew terms for these qualities are *yosher* and *tzedek*.

The first derives from the word *yashar,* upright, straight or honest, while the second originates from the same root as the Hebrew for charity, *tzedaka.* Both indicate the importance of fairness towards others, whether in speech, thought or deed.

From the very beginnings of Judaism the emphasis on justice and fair play as set out in the Torah has created a model which other civilisations have sought to emulate over the centuries. It was Abraham, the first Jew, who pleaded with God to spare the cities of Sodom and Gemorrah, assuming that there were righteous people in them (Genesis 18): "Shall not the Judge of all the earth deal justly?"

Many of the mitzvot bear out the importance of justice and charity — as applied to, for example, fair trials, honest verdicts, weights and measures, business affairs, and dealings between employer and employee. The books of Prophets display great sensitivity to the plight of the orphaned, the widowed and the poor.

The Torah commands: "In *justice* shall you judge your neighbour" (Leviticus 19). The double reference in Deuteronomy 16 — "Justice, justice shall you pursue" — was interpreted to mean that justice should not only be done, but be seen to be done.

The authority to establish a "house of judgement," Beth Din, is contained in the same chapter with the words, "Judges and officers shalt thou make thee." Three qualified rabbis — dayanim — are mandated to act as arbiters in civil disputes and to make decisions on religious matters.

The dayan, or judge, has made a close study of the codes of Jewish law. The Shulchan Aruch enumerates seven requirements expected of a dayan: wisdom, meekness, fear of God, dislike of money, love of truth, love of people, and possession of a good name.

The nineteenth-century Italian scholar, Rabbi Samuel David Luzzatto, wrote in his "Yesodei Ha'torah": "Compassion, which is

"Justice, justice shall you pursue"

the root of love and kindness, is also the source of love, justice and the hatred of violence. From it will emerge a love of righteousness and justice."

Injustice and unkindness were considered by the rabbis to be more heinous than even ritualistic or religious violations. A ritual observance that owed its origin to an injustice had neither merit nor validity (Sanhedrin 6).

Not only judges, of course, are expected to act charitably towards others. Joshua ben Perachya said in the Mishna, "Judge every person meritoriously" (Avot 1), while the Chassidic Rebbe, Mordechai of Neschitz, asserted that charity of mind could bring the most sinful Jew back to the right path. "If you cannot love the transgressor with all your heart, you have not gone even half way towards serving God."

Of the judgement itself, the Torah declares: "You shall do no unrighteousness in judgement. You shall not respect the poor person nor favour the great; you must pass judgement on your neighbour according to justice" (Leviticus 19). Truth alone, not compassion or awe, was to be the overriding factor in reaching a verdict.

In cases brought before a Beth Din, it is usually necessary to provide evidence to prove or disprove a disputed fact. When this is so, at least two witnesses must testify in the same way, as commanded by the Torah: "A single witness cannot suffice to convict a man. The evidence of two witnesses or three is required to sustain the charge" (Deuteronomy 19).

And on the question of false testimony, the Torah adds: "The

judges shall make close inquiry, and if it turns out that the witness who accused his brother is a lying witness [*eid sheker*], you must deal with him as he intended to deal with his brother."

Witnesses in any litigation must fulfil stringent requirements as regards their personal status, their standing in the community and their relationship to the parties concerned.

Judaism teaches that just as people seek righteousness of God, so God demands justice from man. The execution of justice may sometimes seem harsh, but it has to be administered without fear or favour, for "you must be impartial in judgement and give an equal hearing to small and great alike. Do not be afraid of any man, *for the judgement is of God*" (Deuteronomy 1).

Theft/Honesty

A CARDINAL philosophy of Judaism is that one should always be content with one's worldly possessions.

The maxim from *Pirkei Avot* (Ethics of the Fathers) — "Who is rich? The one who rejoices in his portion" — suggests that happiness is dependent on what one has attained for oneself, not on what has been acquired from others through greed or theft. The one who is content in this world will find happiness in the next.

The talmudic sages looked upon theft with particular gravity. They pointed out that Noah's contemporaries committed many evil deeds, but when they turned to robbery and theft there was no alternative but to obliterate those who could not observe even the most basic rules of decency among men (Sanhedrin 108).

Theft is specifically mentioned in the Ten Commandments, where it is interpreted as an act of kidnapping; the prohibition against stealing, on the other hand, is derived from Leviticus 19, where the same verb is used in the plural form, *lo tignovu*, "Ye shall not steal." The same chapter also proscribes burglary in the commandment, "Thou shalt not defraud thy neighbour, nor rob him."

The Hebrew for a thief is *ganav* and for a burglar, *gazlan*. The Talmud suggests a vast difference between the two in Jewish law. The former, who displays more fear of man than of God (doing his utmost not to be seen), must pay double or, in some cases, even fivefold as compensation; the latter, who steals openly and who disdains both man and God equally, is required only to return the article or to repay its value.

The Talmud in tractate Berachot declares that one who does not respond to another person's greeting is termed a *gazlan,* since the person who made the gesture has been robbed of a courteous reply. Stealing is thus not confined to deeds; the prohibition "Ye shall not steal" extends also to thoughts.

It is possible, moreover, to induce people to form a good opinion of oneself through devious means — *genevat da'at,* "stealing the mind" —

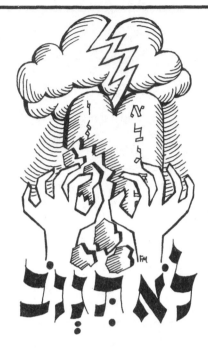

Lo tignov — Thou shalt not steal.

and one is forbidden to act in this way no less in social contact than in business dealings.

Maimonides put it this way: "It is forbidden to cheat people in trade or to deceive them. This rule applies to Jew and non-Jew alike. He who knows that there is a defect in his goods is obliged to bring it to the attention of the purchaser."

Anyone who, for example, invites friends to join him for a holiday knowing full well that the invitation cannot possibly be accepted commits the prohibition of *genevat da'at* by trying to court popularity through deceitful means. Rabbi Samson Raphael Hirsch wrote: "Let a man earn the good opinion of his fellow-man, but let him not steal it."

In today's world the prohibition of *genevat da'at* applies to almost every area of business life. Packaged items are beautifully wrapped for eye-catching sales; imitation jewellery is offered "as good as real"; misleading claims are frequently made in publicity material. An electronic device has even been manufactured to enable a telephone caller to mislead the recipient into thinking, through fabricated background noises, that the call has been dialled from a railway station or airport. All these are examples of "stealing the mind."

Honesty or trust, say the rabbis, is the cornerstone of any society or civilisation. The Lechivitzer Rebbe commented: "We read, 'And ye shall not wrong one another; but you shall fear thy God; for I am the Lord your God' [Leviticus 25]. This means that you shall not deceive one another by asserting that you are a truly God-fearing person."

Aaron Halevi, author of the monumental fourteenth-century "Sefer Hachinuch," said of this verse: "...A cause of decay in civilisation is fraud. Fraudulent dealing results from a person's dissatisfaction with what God has given him and so he lusts for more, even if, by so doing, he has to wrong his fellow-man in order to obtain the objects of his desire."

The saintly Rabbi Israel Salanter (1810-1883), founder of the ethical *musar* movement, often used to supervise the baking of matzot for Pesach. One year he fell ill and his young disciples, wishing to put his mind at rest, asked him to which din (religious law) they should pay particular attention while supervising the baking of the matzot.

Worried that the young men might be carried away by their own enthusiasm, he replied: "There are poor women, even widows, who draw water and knead the dough. Be careful not to grieve them by imposing too much on them. By so doing you would be acting contrary to the moral and ethical teachings of Judaism and would weaken your own mitzva considerably."

The exponents of ethical and moral issues have written numerous works to help improve relations between one person and another. One sinful Jew, they say, can harm an entire people, just as boring a hole under one's own seat in a boat can cause the downfall of the entire crew.

Chastisement of Love

NO ONE can enjoy a life totally bereft of suffering. But Judaism teaches that suffering can be employed as a religious discipline, a spiritual dynamo, if channelled in the right direction, so that pain and sorrow can help to mould one's character.

"I found trouble and sorrow, but I called on the name of the Lord," cried King David (Psalm 116). Although pain and anxiety are unavoidable, they need not bring down a person; on the contrary, on one's journey through life, they can do much to strengthen one's character, if accepted as part of "God's chastenings of love" or the "suffering inflicted by divine love," *yesurim shel ahava* (Berachot 5).

Just as iron and gold have to go through fire and be beaten in order to become toughened and shaped, so the soul sometimes has to undergo a tempest of its own in order to bring out its bearer's nobler aspects.

"My son, despise not the chastening of the Lord, nor spurn his correction; for the Lord corrects him whom He loves, like the father does to the son in whom he delights" (Proverbs 3). Such suffering teaches one humility and compassion, ridding the soul of pride and conceit. It is in this sense that the talmudic expression, *chavivim yesurim,* "suffering is precious" (Baba Metzia 85), is to be understood.

Knowing that sacrifice, suffering and pain are inevitable, the devout Jew places his trust in God, thereby anchoring himself in stormy times. In this he bears in mind another talmudic reference — *kol d'avid rachamana l'tav avid,* "Everything the Merciful One does, He does for good."

In fact, the Talmud, in tractate Berachot, goes out of its way to equate the significance of evil with that of good when it declares: "A person must bless God for all the evil, in the same way as he blesses Him for all the good which befalls him."

The Chasidic Belzer Rebbe once declared that anyone who chanced upon difficult times should realise that God wanted to test him to see how he would react to the situation.

"If you receive the blow with fortitude and repeat the words of Nachum Ish-Gamzu — 'This also is

"... sorrow and tribulation I will find ... and I shall cry out to the Lord"

for my good,' *gam zu l'tova* [as related in tractate Ta'anit 21] — your distress will vanish. There will be no need to try you further and you will then perceive that the misfortune was truly for your good."

The free will, *bechira*, given to man is designed to enable him to take the path that will avoid tribulation and grief. The Torah declares: "See, I have put before you life and death, blessing and curse. Choose life, that both you and your offspring may live" (Deuteronomy 30).

Man himself has to make the choice. He is not a robot or a computer, programmed to live in one way only. He has a choice, and the way he carries out his life is conditioned by the attitude he adopts to his religion and its rules.

Judaism not only teaches one to read Hebrew or translate chapters of the Bible, or even to progress to talmudic studies. It guides young and old alike along the route they should take in order to live a life of blessing and fulfilment, purpose and satisfaction.

As Rabbi Akiva put it: "Although everything is foreseen by God, yet free will is granted to mankind" (Avot 3). Maimonides described free will as the pillar of the Torah and its commandments: "Every person is

capable of being as upright as Moses or as wicked as Jeroboam, wise or foolish, kind or cruel.

"The Creator does not predetermine whether a man should be good or evil, as the foolish astrologers falsely allege; otherwise, what room would there be for the entire Torah?" (Teshuva 5).

A person is able to think and plan ahead, not out of instinct, like an animal, but through choice and freedom of will. His decisions may not always be the correct ones — "For there is not a righteous man on earth who doeth only good and sinneth not," said King Solomon in Ecclesiastes — but the blueprint is given in the Torah, which stresses the true values of Judaism in our daily lives.

The late Chief Rabbi of the Holy Land, Rabbi Abraham Kook, wrote: "The main aim of education is to mould man into his civilised form. Man is civilised if he acts justly and honestly; to educate man to live in that framework is the supreme aim of Jewish religious education.

"Without God and religion, any system or ethical education will lack a solid base and constitutes an unreliable instrument for civilising man" ("Igrot Ha'reiya").

Integrity in Business/Stumbling Block

INTEGRITY in business affairs goes back to the earliest days of our people. Abraham could not get along with his nephew Lot, who was not averse to allowing his flock to graze on other people's land, and the Patriarch was compelled to go his own way rather than work with someone, albeit his own nephew, who had lower ethical standards than his own (Genesis 13).

The following chapter describes Abraham's refusal to take any booty in the victorious Battle of the Kings, while later (Genesis 23) he would not accept as a gift the Cave of Machpelah from Ephron, preferring instead to pay a fair price for the final resting-place of his wife, Sarah.

The Talmud lays great stress on honesty and integrity in business dealings. Tradition has it that in the heavenly tribunal of the next world, the first question asked is: "Were your business affairs conducted in an honest manner?" (Shabbat 31). The term used for correct behaviour is *yashrut b'masah uve'matan,* uprightness in business transactions.

Judaism teaches that a Jew must be a man of his word — his word is his bond. This is particularly so in the case of a promise made to another, which assumes the status of a vow, with the Torah declaring: "That which comes out of your lips you must fulfil" (Deuteronomy 23).

The rabbis stated that one should aim to reach a high level of ethical virtue by fulfilling a decision made mentally — such as giving a charitable gift — even if no promise was uttered verbally. This lesson is derived from the verse, "He who speaks the truth in his heart . . ." (Psalms 15).

The talmudic term, *echad b'peh v'echad b'lev* — "The mouth and the heart are one" (Pesachim 113) — makes clear that hypocrisy is sinful and that the way one speaks and the way one thinks should coincide. Nor should one mislead a buyer by using terms which misconstrue the real meaning of a statement.

Two men once came to the Chasidic Premishlaner Rebbe to ask his advice on the wisdom of forming a partnership. The rabbi took a piece of paper, wrote down the first four letters of the Hebrew alphabet, and said: "This can be your contract.

"Aleph stands for *emunah* (faith), bet for *berachah* (blessing), gimel for *geneivah* (stealing), and daled for *dalut* (poverty). In other words, if you have faith in each other and are honest, the outcome will be a blessing; but should you treat each other dishonestly and carelessly, then the venture can only result in poverty and disaster."

The Torah continually emphasises the emotional and financial effects a misleading statement or action can have. From the verse, "And you shall not put a stumbling-block before a blind man" (Leviticus 19), the rabbis deduce not only the literal meaning, but also the harm that can follow by introducing unsuspecting people to drugs, obscene books or dubious places of entertainment, or by offering, for example, non-kosher food to an observant Jew.

To suggest a course of action known to be contrary to someone's interests also comes under the category of "putting a stumbling-block before the blind." The author of the fourteenth-century "Sefer Ha'chinuch," Aaron Halevi, comments: "There are three pillars on which the world is established — truth, mutual confidence and mutual trust. Without these, society could not survive."

The Torah warns against encroaching on another person's property, which it ranks with robbery and theft. "You shall not remove your neighbour's landmark," it warns in Deuteronomy 19, later including this prohibition in the list of curses enumerated by the Levites on Mount Ebal: "Cursed be he who removes his neighbour's landmark".

By way of extension, the rabbis included encroachment, *hasagat gevul,* among any unfair methods used in the commercial, financial or spiritual interests of a second party. To jeopardise a person's livelihood through unfair competition, infringement of copyright or plagiarism is considered as trespassing on his property.

Although the original prohibition referred to the boundary-stones which marked off one man's field from that of his neighbour, the moral issues are equally applicable to today's world.

Local councils or chambers of commerce ensure that shops of a similar nature are not allowed to open too near to each other; advertisers have to maintain a strict code of conduct in order not to mislead potential buyers; and the creation of monopolies is discouraged.

"Put not a stumbling block before the blind"

Clean/Obscene Speech. Flattery

THE SAME letters that can produce a Bible or an inspiring speech can also be used to create an indecent book or an obscene statement. The choice is ours.

The talmudic sages placed great emphasis on the sanctity of speech, *kedushat halashon,* and the written word. The use of coarse and vulgar words is considered a grave transgression, for which there are severe penalties (Shabbat 33, Ketubot 8), and the rabbis admonish us to be discriminating in our use of words and to express ourselves in a refined manner.

On the contemporary front, when the world of entertainment and the mass media depict a society which has seemingly descended to the abyss of moral degradation, the necessity to heed the words of the rabbis is stronger than ever. It is at times such as this, says the Torah, that we must raise the standards of sanctity and morality in our everyday lives.

Nor should the power of the pen and of speech be under-estimated. "Death and life are in the hands of the tongue," says Proverbs 18, to which King David added in Psalm 34: "Guard your tongue from evil."

Speech and writing are a significant yardstick to measure the character and stature of a person. God has given us the power of speech and it is our duty to use this gift to the best of our ability.

"The words of the wise are listened to with pleasure," says Ecclesiastes, because they are uttered with consideration and humility. As Rabbi Avtalyon warned: "Sages, be careful with words!" (Avot 1), from which the Talmud deduces that if sages and wise men are to be heedful of their words, how much more careful should be those who are not sages and are not so wise?

Rabbi Yisrael Salanter told his followers that, before speaking, they should always ask themselves, "Is what I am about to say really necessary and useful?" Often, silence is preferable. And he added: "Try not to speak all you think, nor write down all you say. It is easy to speak and to write, but difficult to forget a vicious word once spoken, and even harder to obliterate the written word."

In Judaism, holiness is not an abstract concept, but one which governs day-to-day life. Anything unclean, barbaric or irrational is abhorred; and this applies no less to speech than it does to personal hygiene or the way one is dressed.

Lashon nekiya, clean and refined speech, helps to uphold the very basis of our heritage. It shows consideration not only for oneself, but also for those who have to hear or read what we have said or written.

Tone of voice and manner of speech are equally important, particularly to children, who often mimic their elders, and once a habit is formed, it is difficult to break. Said Maimonides: "A man's character is what habit makes it."

Ibn Gabirol, the medieval scholar, wrote in his "The Choice of Pearls": "If I utter a word, it becomes my master; but should I not utter it, I am its master." However, "it is better to speak (the truth) than to maintain silence" and "those who are able to make the right use of speech are able to make the right use of silence."

The sages denounce the flatterer, *chanfan,* throughout the Talmud. Of his wily ways, King Solomon cautioned: "He who says to the wicked, 'You are righteous,' people shall curse him, nations shall denounce him" (Proverbs 24). Flattery prompted by desire for personal favours is to be avoided at all costs.

The fifteenth-century ethical work, "Orchot Tzaddikim," lists nine categories of flattery and concludes that a person is influenced, in thought and deeds, by the company he keeps and by the habits of those among whom he lives. It suggests, therefore, that one should choose one's friends and companions with care and associate only with the righteous and wise.

"If you have friends, some of whom praise you and some of whom correct and rebuke you, love the ones who rebuke you, and hate the ones who praise you, for the ones who rebuke you are conducting you to life eternal, and those who praise you will rejoice in your misfortune even though they praise you" (Avot d'Rabbi Nathan, 29).

Flattery, *chanufa,* causes a person to be repugnant to God, as stated in the verse, "Lying lips are an abomination to the Eternal" (Proverbs 12). Rabbeinu Bachya, in his "Kad ha'Kemach," states that we should follow the example of Noah, Abraham and Jacob, all of whom were termed "wholehearted" in the sense that they conducted their lives in a sincere and exemplary manner.

There are, however, occasions when flattery is permissible. The Chasidic Koretser Rebbe said that "flattery is forgiveable only if it promotes peace," and the Midrash stated: "A man may flatter his wife for the sake of peace and harmony; his creditor in order to get an extension; and his teacher in order to get special attention."

But, generally, our sages frowned on any form of flattery, cynicism, scorn and scoffing, since these were regarded as a barrier to wisdom and knowledge.

Shaming Another/Gratitude

TO SHAME a person in public, *halbanat panim,* is, said the rabbis, one of the gravest offences of all. The Talmud states: "Let a man throw himself into a blazing furnace rather than shame another person in public" (Berachot 43).

In another reference, it compares this offence to murder: "Shaming another in public is like shedding blood" (Baba Metzia 58). This form of degradation is as serious as *shefichat damim,* bloodshed, since any kind of embarrassment or indignity is, indeed, tantamount to psychological or spiritual murder.

The literal meaning of the Hebrew term for shaming is, in fact, "to make white the face [of a fellow human being]"; when one is publicly insulted and disgraced, "the red (blood) recedes and whiteness appears" (one becomes deathly pale).

Since man is considered to be an image or reflection of the Almighty, any act committed against another, be it physical or psychological, is regarded as a desecration of God's sanctity and a rebellion against His authority. The sages therefore stress the care and sensitivity that must be taken to safeguard the feelings of a fellow human being.

It was, says the Talmud, just such an incident which led to the destruction of the Second Temple. A well-known dignitary had sent out invitations to a banquet, including one to his good friend, Kamza. The invitation, however, was inadvertently addressed to one Bar Kamza, who was, in fact, an enemy of the host.

During the banquet, the celebrant spotted the mistake and ordered Bar Kamza to leave his home. The guest pleaded with the host not to humiliate him and even offered to pay for the cost of the banquet. But the host, devoid of feeling, was adamant, seized Bar Kamza and threw him out.

Full of rage — particularly since many sages who were present did nothing to stop the indignity — Bar Kamza went to the Roman ruler and told him the tale. This, said the rabbis, set in motion the chain of events which eventually led to the destruction of the Second Temple (Gittin 55).

One rabbi of the Mishna, Elazar of

Modin, asserted that, even if a person was well-versed in the Torah and performed many kindnesses, "If he insults his fellow man in public, he has no share in the world to come" (Avot 3). And the Midrash added: "A person can be killed only once; but when he is shamed, he is killed many times over" (Eliyahu 42).

The Torah stresses that if we wish to point out a fault to a friend or neighbour, it should be done in such a way as not to cause any shame: "You shall surely rebuke your neighbour (with tact and delicacy) and not cause sin because of him" (Leviticus 19).

A perception of shame is a vital requisite in the formation of a worthy character. A bold or shameless person, one who ignores public disapproval, is a genuine threat to communal harmony. The Hebrew term for arrogance, *chutzpa,* indicates impudence allied to shamelessness and it received strong condemnation from the rabbis.

There is, however, shame that brings sin and shame that brings glory. Solomon Ibn Gabirol placed shame at the top of a list of ten virtues, while Bachya Ibn Pakuda says that "many precepts of the Torah are fulfilled not because of piety, but out of a sense of shame."

Many customs are observed in order not to differentiate between poor and rich, thereby obviating any cause for embarrassment; the custom of the bride not wearing any jewellery under the chupa is one example. In Temple times, on the fifteenth of Av and on Yom Kippur, the unmarried girls of Jerusalem danced in the vineyards in unadorned white dresses so that rich and poor would look alike (Mishna Ta'anit 4).

The avoidance of this kind of shame, *busha,* is no less important when giving charity, so that one does not hurt the feelings of the recipient, or when giving advice or information to one who is less learned than oneself; in either case we should respond by putting the recipient at ease.

One of the first Hebrew sentences taught to a child opens with the words, *modeh ani l'fanecha ...,* " I give thanks to Thee, O King, who is eternal ...," recited when rising each morning. The day starts with a prayer of thanks and the child is educated to appreciate good health, a loving home and caring parents.

The Hebrew for gratitude, *hakarat tova,* of acknowledging every favour and kindness, provides a principle that is at the very foundation of Judaism. The Ten Commandments begin not with words about the Creation, but with the statement: "I am the Lord your God, who brought you out from the Land of Egypt" (Exodus 20) — with miracles and wonders, from servitude to freedom.

"For this," asserts the Midrash, "you must be grateful and thereby accept the kingship of Heaven" (Mishnat R. Eliezer 137). Gratitude is thus an obligation, manifested in observance of the mitzvot, which, say the rabbis, were given for the elevation of mankind.

In Temple times thanksgiving sacrifices were offered up on joyous occasions, and today our prayers include blessings not only for special events, but also for any benefits we may enjoy, beautiful sights or new clothes. Nothing is taken for granted.

The renowned first-century Jewish philosopher, Philo Judaeus, wrote: "Let no one, however humble and insignificant, despairing of a better fortune, scruple to become a supplicant of God. Even if he expects nothing more, let him give thanks to the best of his power for what he has already received. Infinite are the gifts he has: birth, life, nature, soul, sensation, imagination, desire, reason."

As an old Yiddish folk saying puts it: "We never know all we should be grateful for."

Dispute/Argument. Judge in scale of merit

THE BLESSING which exceeds all other human virtues is that of peace and harmony. Yet Judaism recognises human weaknesses, that there are bound to be differences of opinion between people.

This is, after all, a natural, even desirable, phenomenon. It creates discussion and motivates competition. In certain cases it even stimulates wisdom.

But, say our sages, disputes or arguments must not be self-seeking. It is the cause or ideal which matters and we are urged to follow the example of Hillel and Shammai, who, despite their many differences, nevertheless remained the best of friends.

Their disputes came under the category of *machaloket leshem shamayim*, "differences for the sake of heaven." Not for personal gain or glory did they argue; they differed because they wanted to give what they each believed to be the true meaning of the Torah.

The Talmud relates that a heavenly voice was heard to say, "Both Hillel and Shammai speak the words of the one living God."

The Mishna, giving an example of a dispute caused solely through personal ambition, cites the rebellion of Korach and his company against the authority of Moses and Aaron. This kind of dispute, it says, is bound to meet with a tragic end (Avot 5).

Controversy can have permanent value only when there is a common aim, without any selfish motive. Maimonides declared that when the purpose of an argument was not to contradict, but rather to persuade another to accept the truth, this kind of intellectual give-and-take would inevitably result in an amicable settlement that would endure forever.

Judaism has many customs designed to avoid confrontation and strife. Certain honours, such as being called up to the first portion of the reading of the Torah, are given to a Cohen, thereby forestalling any congregant who may feel he has a

prior claim to this privilege.

The Torah stresses that personal disputes must be settled by law or arbitration: "If there be a controversy between men ... the judges shall judge them ..." (Deuteronomy 25).

Machaloket, argument that causes friction and unpleasantness, whether on a personal or communal level, must be avoided or brought to a speedy conclusion at all costs. The example was set by Abraham, who separated from his nephew, Lot, in order to avoid strife (Genesis 13).

A leading authority in the Holy Land, Rabbi Isaiah Horowitz (1570-1626), advised: "Keep away from strife, and if it is started, it should be extinguished immediately" (Shelah 1, page 280).

Disputes often arise because a person has been misunderstood or has not been given the benefit of the doubt. The rabbis cautioned that one should be charitable in his opinions of others, *dan lechaf zechut,* taken from the sayings of Joshua ben Perachyah, "Judge all men charitably" (Avot 1).

Nor should we jump to conclusions. Appearances are often misleading, and suspicion can lead to unwarranted hatred.

Rabbi Isaiah Horowitz wrote: "To judge every man in the scale of merit, to give people the benefit of the doubt, is a praiseworthy quality. It avoids strife and dissention and leads to peace on earth. The one who practises

this ethical maxim is himself judged by God in the scale of merit.

"If one lacks this virtue and suspects others, he will himself be suspected by others. If, however, one feels that his friend should be severely criticised for Heaven's sake, then it is his duty to do so" (Shelah 1).

The Torah commands: "In righteousness shall you judge your neighbour" (Leviticus 19); in other words, one should try to balance the pros and cons of a case in favour of merit, *zechut,* rather than find fault and subsequently condemn.

One can never be sure of the circumstances of a particular situation, or of the stresses and strains which induce certain statements or actions. Sometimes we are not told of the circumstances, but sometimes we don't think and fail to appreciate the consequences of our thoughtlessness.

Hillel, who rose from the ranks to the highest rabbinical position on the Sanhedrin, was a man of refined character, kind and peaceful by nature. He advised: "Do not judge your fellow man until you have been in his position" (Avot 2).

A Chasidic rebbe renowned for his benevolent approach to others, Levi Yitzchak of Berditchev, once met a young man smoking on Shabbat.

"You must have forgotten that today is the Sabbath day," said the rabbi. "No," came the reply, "I am fully aware of it." "Then perhaps you don't know that it is forbidden to smoke on the Sabbath?" "I do know!" the man replied. "Then it must be that your doctor prescribed smoking as a remedy, and that is the reason for your profaning the Sabbath?" the rabbi inquired patiently.

Smiling, the man replied: "Not at all." At this point, the rabbi could no longer contain himself, raised his hands heavenwards and declared: "Lord of the Universe, see how honest your children are! Rather than tell a lie, they will admit anything. How can You not have compassion and pity on them?"

Shabbat (Sabbath)

AND GOD BLESSED the seventh day and declared it holy, because on it He had ceased from all His work of creation which He had done. (Gen. 2:3)

The observance of the Sabbath day was the very first commandment with which the Children of Israel were charged even before the Giving of the Torah at Mount Sinai which, of course, included the Ten Commandments and the observance of Sabbath which bears witness to the creation of the universe. Above all other days of the Jewish calendar, the Sabbath is unique in so many ways that its teachings are exhilarating to the extreme if we understand its beauty and its beneficial effects on the lives of those who observe its precepts, traditions and customs.

The fourth of the Ten Commandants has been accepted by the whole of civilisation as enjoining a weekly day of rest, separated from the working weekday by the two basic motifs of rest and holiness. This produces a sacred feeling, uplifting the individual from the mundane activities of the other six days of the week.

From the moment that the lady of the house ushers in the Sabbath by the lighting of the candles, until the conclusion of the Sabbath at sundown the next day, there is an atmosphere of peace and tranquility which can only be appreciated by those who actually observe and experience the weekly Sabbath day.

Preparations for this holy day commence almost as soon as we end the previous Sabbath, in thought and deed we anticipate the oasis in the day-to-day activities of the week. By the time that Sabbath arrives, the family look smart in their best clothing, with the home brightly prepared with a white tablecloth, lit candles, two *Challot* (white loaves), and the *Kiddush* cup and wine, waiting for the return of those who have attended the *Kabbalat Shabbat* (inauguration of the Sabbath) service in the synagogue. Psalms and references to Israel's return to Zion are included in the Sabbath Eve service. On arrival home, the children are blessed by the parents and a special hymn of praise from the Book of Proverbs about the valiant wife and mother is sung.

Being a relaxing day, there is more time for singing, both in the home and in the synagogue. In between the courses during meal time, *Zemirot* (table hymns) are sung to texts which allude to Biblical and Midrashic literature, creating a joyous expression of sublime peace and harmony in the home. The synagogue services include extra Psalms and prayers sung by the congregation in the musical mode (*Nusach*) which identifies it with one of the five services of the Sabbath day.

It was the prophet Isaiah who first spoke about the physical and spiritual blessings which this day brings expressing it thus "... and call the Sabbath a delight" (Isaiah 58:13). The physical and spiritual blessings are highlighted on this unique day of the week by eating and drinking more than any other day, being reminded about the Creation and the many kindnesses of the Almighty, and through special prayers, hymns and ceremonies.

Those attending the Sabbath morning service in the synagogue will participate in the recitation of blessings for the leaders and supporters of the community, for the Royal Family, and for the government, as well as for the welfare of the State of Israel — texts which date back both to Talmudic times and to recent decades.

The principal feature of the Sabbath is its holiness created by every aspect of life on that day. Even how a person walks should be different and more relaxed than during the rest of the week. The family should be enjoying each other's company in study and discussion; in visitation of relatives and friends; and in friendliness and thoughtfulness towards other people, continuing into the following week.

It is a day which can improve the character of the person, by the discipline of the obedience to the Torah commands to refrain from all productive activity on this sacred day whilst at the same time acknowledging the fact that there is a Creator who knows best what is good for humans as stated: "The seventh day is to be a Sabbath to the Lord your God ...", followed by: "On it you shall not do any kind of work." (Exodus 20:10) Through its observance we create self-control over our activities which bring us to a higher spiritual plane, making us realise the purpose of life and how we should live our lives to the full, being motivated by the ideals of the Sabbath day — peace and harmony. The Hebrew word *Shabbat* means "cessation of work" and through that act we abandon our domination over the world and its resources giving time for reflection and meditation away from the hustle and bustle of the weekday routine.

The Sabbath day is ushered in by a blessing, over wine, *Kiddush*, and the holiness of this special day concludes with another blessing over wine during a ritual which also includes blessings over spices and a burning flame, *Havdalah*. These are symbolic acts which remind the Jew that by the observance of the commandments an example will be given of the ultimate purpose of the Jewish people, which is that of being "a light unto the nations."

Rosh Hashana (New Year)

IT IS NOT without coincidence that the human faculties — the powers of the mind and body — are centred within the head (*rosh* in Hebrew). When we use our heads wisely, we can plan for the future.

We call the New Year *Rosh Hashana,* "head of the year," for much the same reason. The very name indicates the serious and sacred purpose of the day, when the Jew is encouraged to think seriously about the nature of the year that lies ahead.

During Ellul we have had time to review the past year, to recognise and rectify any shortcomings in our behaviour. We can look forward to the coming year with an optimism rooted in the opportunity we have had to mend our ways.

Says the Almighty: "See, I have set before you this day life and good, and death and evil . . . the blessing and the

curse; therefore *choose life* that you may live, you and your children, to love the Lord your God, to listen to His voice and to cleave to Him" (Deuteronomy 30).

The principle of free will is fundamental to Judaism. "It is," says Maimonides, "the pillar of the Law and of the commandments."

Man is his own master and in his hands lies his destiny. Much depends, of course, on both home environment and outside influence, but the choice of what to do rests, in the final analysis, with the individual himself.

During the very first meal of the New Year round chalot are used instead of square or twisted ones, to indicate the unity of God. Just as a circle has no beginning or end, so is God eternal. The shape also reminds one of a crown, of the kingship of the Almighty — a theme employed throughout the High Holy-days.

Instead of sprinkling salt over the chala, the bread is dipped into honey, to express hope for a sweet and good year. The numerical value of *dvash,* (honey) is 306, the same as that of *av harachamim,* Father of Mercy.

As a first course it is customary to eat the head of a fish, with the brief prayer: "May the coming year bring about our reaching the head (of society) and not its tail." The commentator Abudraham remarks that just as fish multiply rapidly, so should our merits be increasingly manifest.

Similarly, pomegranates are eaten, symbolic of the hope that our meritorious deeds will be as great as the number of seeds in this fruit.

During the meal the traditional dish of tzimmas, made of carrots, sweet potatoes and honey, symbolises our prayers for a good year. Honey cake and honey biscuits similarly help to bring sweetness and joy into the solemnity of the occasion.

The name Rosh Hashana is nowhere to be found in the Bible. The festival is known as *zikaron,* a memorial, or *teruah,* blowing of the shofar (Leviticus 23). But since the first of Tishri is the day when mankind is judged, says the Talmud, it became

known as the beginning of the year. It was also the day when the *shemita* (sabbatical year) and *yovel* (jubilee year) began.

The main obligation regarding the shofar is to *hear* its sounds: it is this call of the shofar which arouses the Jew to repentance.

The wearing of the kittel, the white gown under the talit, serves as a reminder of both purity and festivity. It takes us back to Temple times, when the High Priest wore white while serving in the Holy of Holies.

The first afternoon of Rosh Hashana concludes with the ritual of tashlich, "casting away," derived from the verse in Micah, "You shall cast all their sins into the depths of the sea." Psalms and prayers are recited by the banks of running water, after which one's pockets are emptied in a symbolic act signifying the intention to cast away sin.

Just as the fish have no eyelids with which to close their eyes, so our knowledge that God has an ever-seeing eye should forever deter us from committing evil. A fish swims everywhere, yet can suddenly become entrapped; similarly, the Jew should be alert enough not to be trapped by temptation that can suddenly be sprung on him.

The ten days of penitence (*aseret yemei teshuva*) that precede Yom Kippur include Shabbat Shuva, which takes its name from the haftara of that day. It is the custom for the minister to give a special sermon in which he emphasises the significance of the High Holy-days.

Yom Kippur (Day of Atonement)

THE VERY MENTION of Yom Kippur, the Sabbath of Sabbaths, is enough to instil a feeling of awe and reverence in all but the least devout of Jews. Well before the fast itself, both home and synagogue assume a spirit of solemnity not experienced at any other time of the year.

Immediately after the morning service on Yom Kippur eve, the ritual of *hatarat nedarim,* absolution of vows, takes place among groups of four or more worshippers. Three act as a Beth Din and the fourth is the supplicant, who recites a Hebrew formula cancelling any vows towards God which, for one reason or another, were not fulfilled. Each member of the group in turn assumes the role of supplicant.

Another pre-Yom Kippur custom is the *kapparot* (expiation) ceremony, during which prayers are recited while one holds a fowl or money that is waved around the head three times before being given to the poor. *Kappara* is achieved, says the *unetanei tokef* prayer, by repentance, prayer and charity.

The *mincha* (afternoon) service is held earlier than usual to allow for proper preparation for the fast. It includes the confessional *al chet* recited during all subsequent services on Yom Kippur. With a clenched right fist we beat the heart at the mention of each "For the sin" of the 44 sins listed.

The list, known as the Great Confession (*vidui raba*), consists of pairs of lines starting with consecutive Hebrew letters. The shorter form of confession (*vidui zuta*), beginning with the word *ashamnu.* is a series of single words in aleph-bet sequence, plus two extra words for the last letter, making a total of 24 words. It is recited ten times on Yom Kippur.

On the eve of the fast one is commanded to eat more than usual at the last meal, the *seuda hamafseket.* Our sages said: "Eating and drinking on the eve of Yom Kippur are equivalent to fasting on Yom Kippur" (Berachot 8).

Yom Kippur is, in fact, a festival, but since we are commanded to fast, the food we would normally eat on a festival is consumed during the meal preceding it. The festive spirit of the day is described in the Talmud, which relates how girls would put on white dresses and go out into the fields to sing and dance.

Before leaving for synagogue for the Kol Nidre service, it is customary to bless one's children and then to light the festival candles, as well as an additional memorial candle which burns throughout Yom Kippur.

"A lamp of the Lord," says Proverbs, "is the soul of man." This day is referred to in rabbinic literature as *yom hakippurim* (in the plural), which suggests that we ask God for forgiveness not only for the living, but also for those who have gone to their eternal rest.

One is forbidden to wear leather shoes on Yom Kippur and these are removed and replaced by sandals or slippers before Kol Nidre starts.

The congregation assembles well before sunset, Kol Nidre being the only time in the year when the male worshippers wear a talit in the evening. Since the blessing for the talit may be recited only while it is still light, the service begins before nightfall.

It commences with the opening of the Ark, with the Torah scrolls being carried to the centre of the synagogue and the chazan reciting the verse, "Light is sown to the righteous, and gladness for the upright in heart" (Psalm 97: 11). All can find the light of understanding through a return to the ways of the Torah.

The *musaf* (additional) service on the following day includes the *avoda,* the order of service in the sanctuary, which describes the Yom Kippur ritual of High Priest and congregation as outlined in the Talmud. This was the one day in the year when the High Priest entered the Holy of Holies in the Temple, having studied all the details involved in the atonement ceremony.

The vivid description of the *avoda* is couched in emotional terms and is chanted in such a way as to stir the innermost feelings of the worshipper. Many congregants participate physically by kneeling with the chazan during those sections that recall the High Priest's ministrations in the sanctuary.

Yom Kippur ends as it began: the Ark is opened and the congregation recites the *shema Yisrael* and other verses of equal import. "When we recite these verses, with great reverence and in a loud and clear voice, we resolve to dedicate our lives anew to the glory of God," said the Sh'la, Rabbi Horowitz of Prague.

The link is maintained, for immediately we fulfil another religious obligation — that of preparing to make the succa in order to act on the verse in Psalm 84, "They go from strength to strength."

Succot (Tabernacles)

THE CULMINATION of this festive period is Succot, *z'man simchateinu*, the season of our rejoicing: to "serve the Lord with joy" (Psalm 100) is a fundamental principle of our faith.

The mitzvot of this festival stand to remind us of God's eternal love and mercy and of our consequent need to be grateful to Him for the goodness with which mankind is blessed.

For 40 years the Israelites wandered in the wilderness before reaching the Promised Land. Thus we celebrate *chag hasuccot*, the festival of tabernacles, the third of the pilgrim festivals.

Why is Succot not celebrated in the month the Exodus took place, Nissan, rather than in Tishri? Because, say the commentators, it would not be unpleasant to stay in the succah during the springtime, when it is warm; on the other hand, in the autumn it is often rainy, and the Jew dwells in the booth because he was commanded to do so in the Torah, despite the fact that he may have to experience some discomfort.

This season also marks the end of the harvest and thus takes on the name *chag ha'asif*, the festival of the ingathering, which was a time of pride and joy to the farmer for the successful completion of his work over a period of months.

The laws regarding the construction, content and materials of the succah convey valuable lessons on how to behave in life. For example, the succah must be more shaded than exposed to the rays of the sun: similarly, a person should not allow good fortune alone to influence his qualities and character.

Nor should the tabernacle be too high (above twenty cubits) or too low (below ten handbreaths), teaching man not to be too haughty and arrogant or too humble and meek. The walls must be firm enough to withstand normal gusts of wind; so must a person not be excessively shaken by sad or joyous events in his life.

Besides the commandment to "dwell in the booth" there is the ritual of the *arba'a minim*, the four species (Leviticus 23) — the *etrog* (citrus), *lulav* (palm branch), *hadassim* (myrtles) and *aravot* (willows). The commentator Abudraham explains why these four species are held together during the recitation of the blessing and the *na'anuim*, the waving in six directions.

The etrog, he says, has both taste and scent; likewise there are Jews who are both educated in the ways of the Torah and strict in its observance. The fruit of the palm has taste, but no fragrance; so there are Jews who are learned in Torah, but are devoid of good deeds and do not pass on their knowledge.

The hadass has scent, but no taste; so are there people who perform good deeds, but are not knowledgeable. And the arava has neither scent nor taste, corresponding to those who are both ignorant and selfish.

If, however, we bind all four together, the more virtuous may protect and complement those who lack such qualities. Only in this conjoined position can the appropriate blessing be made.

"Just as a person cannot fulfil his obligation on the festival of tabernacles unless all *arba'a minim* are held together, so Israel can be redeemed only when all Israel hold together and are united" (Yalkut Shimoni 188a).

In the old community of Slonim, so it is told, it was the custom for anyone who had bought an etrog to obtain the opinion of Rabbi Eizel Harif as to its suitability. One year the rabbi refused to approve any of the etrogim shown to him.

When the etrog dealer heard about this, he remonstrated angrily with the rabbi, claiming that the financial loss involved would jeopardise his family's welfare for the entire year. The rabbi, upset that he might be the cause of the dealer's suffering, replied: "It is true that your etrogim are unsuitable and when my judgement is asked, I must tell the truth.

"God forbid, however, that I should cause a Jew to suffer. I suggest, therefore, that you give every buyer two etrogim instead of one. When they come to ask me which one of the two is superior, I will be able to answer in all honesty that one is better than the other and so your sales will not suffer."

Shemini Atzeret and Simchat Torah

FOR OVER a month, additional prayers and psalms have been added to the synagogue services. Since the first days of Selichot, followed by Rosh Hashana, the ten days of penitence (*aseret yemei teshuva*), Yom Kippur and Succot, the Jew has been engrossed in religious activity which has elevated him to a spiritual plane higher than at any other time of the year.

In reaching these heights God has come closer to him and for this reason the Almighty has added an extra day, Shemini Atseret (the Eighth Day of Solemn Assembly), to the sequence of festive days.

God, said our sages, is likened to a king who invites his children to a celebration lasting a predetermined number of days. When they are due to go, He tells them: "I hate to see you go — please stay one more day." Having been guests in the house of the Lord for so many weeks, the Torah commands us, yet again, to be joyful.

Shemini Atseret is a separate festival from that of Succot. The *shehecheyanu* blessing is therefore recited again both when the yomtov candles are lit and when kiddush is recited.

A special prayer for rain (*tefilat geshem*) is added during the musaf section of the morning service. The period chosen for this prayer, after the harvest and the season of dwelling in the succah, reflects the agricultural requirements and weather conditions of Eretz Israel. Its recitation by Jews throughout the globe helps to heighten their awareness of the land and maintain their links with Israel.

The prayer was composed in the sixth century by Rabbi Eleazar Hakalir, the author of many liturgical poems and hymns. A native of Eretz Israel, he employed the theme of *zechut avot,* the "merit of the fathers" — the Patriarchs, Moses, Aaron and the twelve tribes of Israel — to plead for rain and sustenance. A similar theme runs through all the prayers for atonement and forgiveness on Yom Kippur.

The finale of this holy and joyous season is Simchat Torah, the Rejoicing of the Law. Mentioned neither in the Torah nor in the Talmud, it evolved some time in the

eleventh century as the second day of Shemini Atseret. (In Israel, Shemini Atseret and Simchat Torah are celebrated on the same day.)

However, the custom of reading the final portion of the Torah on this day was established in the Talmud. The reading of Genesis, chapter one, was introduced some time after the twelfth century to indicate that "just as we are privileged to witness its [the Torah's] completion, so shall we be privileged to witness its beginning."

Self-denial is not encouraged in Judaism. "The Divine Presence (the *shechina*)," says the Talmud, "rests only with those who *joyfully* perform the commandments of the Torah." To underline this, we end the series of festivals on the happiest note of the year — by concluding and recommencing the annual cycle of reading the Torah.

The study of God's word, our rabbis teach us, knows no end. It is a constant process of education and research into the vast sea of Jewish literature, accumulated over the

thousands of years and based on the Torah, the most honoured and sacred possession of the Jew.

The Chasidic Rabbi of Ger once asked a young man if he had learned Torah. "Just a little," replied the youth. "That," said the rabbi, "is all anyone has ever learned of the Torah."

On Simchat Torah the ceremonial circuits, *hakafot,* are made around the synagogue — with the Torah scrolls borne aloft — during the evening and morning services. Circuits are first mentioned in the Bible in connection with the downfall of Jericho. Later, during the seven days of Succot, the lulav and aravot were carried in the Temple, a custom perpetuated to this day in the procession round the synagogue.

Children play a prominent role in the Simchat Torah proceedings, carrying flags and marching like soldiers behind the Torah-bearers. The "Sefer Ha'taamim" says that this is to impress on them that all Israel are God's army and that our only battle is for the Torah.

After every member of the congregation has been called up to the reading of the Law, the children are gathered on to the bima for the ceremony of *kol hane'arim,* "all the youngsters." They listen to the reading of a portion from the Torah, having recited the appropriate blessing accompanied by an adult.

Those honoured to complete and restart the reading of the Law are the *Chatan Torah,* bridegroom of the Law, and *Chatan Bereshit,* bridegroom of Genesis. The word *chatan* suggests that the Jew is wedded to the Torah, that he should study it and always observe its teachings.

In fact, during the reading of these portions, a large talit is held over the bima like a chupa at a wedding. Both occasions share the same spirit of festivity and joy, as expressed in the words of the prayer sung before returning the scrolls to the Ark: "Be glad and rejoice on this Festival of Rejoicing of the Law."

Chanucah (Feast of Lights)

THE BATTLE of the few against the many, the weak against the strong, has confronted the Jewish people throughout its history. Yet the only festival in our calendar which centres on a military victory is Chanucah.

Even the celebration itself, however, concerns not so much that of victory as the rededication of the defiled Temple. War and strife have no place in Judaism; whether in the home or in the world at large, the stress is on *shalom*, peace.

But there are times when civil rights and religious freedom are at stake and when there is no alternative but to fight for these rights. The story of Chanucah is the story of one such battle, and the legacy of the Maccabees has served as a shining example over two millenia.

Chanucah does not start on the date of a great battle, or on the anniversary of the conquest of Jerusalem. It marks the time when a single cruse of oil, normally sufficient for only one day's lighting of the Temple menora, miraculously lasted for eight days, by which time fresh oil had been prepared (Talmud, Shabbat 21).

The sages ruled that for eight days Hallel, psalms and prayers of thanksgiving be recited, though no festive feast is prescribed. The Chasidic Rebbe of Ger was asked why Chanucah lacked what Purim had. He replied: "On Purim we celebrate the annulment of the royal decree to destroy the body, so we partake of a meal to give pleasure to the body. On Chanucah, however, Antiochus of Syria sought to destroy the Jewish soul, and on being rescued we recite suitable psalms to gratify our soul."

The Book of Esther relates that Haman conspired "to exterminate, slaughter and destroy all Jews"; Antiochus, on the other hand, desired to make the Jews "forgetful of thy Torah" and to force them to transgress "the statutes of thy will."

Chanucah means "dedication," but it can be divided to read *chanu*, "they rested," and *cah*, which adds up to 25 (in other words, "they rested on the 25th of Kislev.") The festival is also called Chag Ha'urim, the Feast of Lights, and the menora should always be kindled near a window or door, "to

proclaim and publicise" the miracle to passers by.

The candles should be kindled preferably at the appearance of the stars. Each day one more is added and the new candle is always lit first. The central candle that kindles the others is called the *shamash*, "servant," and is the only one which may provide light for other purposes (Shabbat 22).

So important is the mitzva of lighting the candles, say the rabbis, that everything must be done to obtain the necessary candles or oil.

The Sachatchover Rebbe, Rabbi Avraham Bornstein (1830-1910), was asked why the Shulchan Aruch insists that one must buy Chanucah candles even if destitute, whereas other commandments are not obligatory for those who lack the means. He replied: "The Talmud states that if one is contemplating performing a mitzva, but is unintentionally prevented from doing so, the Creator allocates this person the credit of actually having done the deed" (Berachot 6).

"Chanucah candles, however, are lit in order to give public testimony to the great miracles associated with the festival. Mere intention cannot give public evidence, so this particular precept can be fulfilled only by actual performance."

During the week of Chanucah, it is customary to focus attention on children — the Hebrew words for dedication and education derive from the same root. Special events take place which enhance the study of the Torah among children and youth; family games, such as playing with the dreidl, are encouraged, particularly while the candles are alight, since no work may be carried out during that time.

The dreidl (or *s'vivon*) is made to spin from above, while the *ra'ashon*, the greger used on Purim, is spun from below. This indicates that the miracle of Chanucah rotated around heavenly matters (spirit and soul), whereas the Purim miracle revolved around earthly matters (body and life).

The sages point to various biblical allusions to Chanucah. They note that the twenty-fifth word in the Torah is *or*, "light," and that the twenty-fifth location where the Children of Israel encamped during their wanderings in the wilderness was Hasmonah.

The eternal message of the Hasmoneans is summarised in the words of the prophet Zechariah, read on Shabbat Chanucah: "Not by might, nor by power, but by My spirit, saith the Lord of Hosts."

Fast Days

FOR 850 YEARS, from the day Joshua led the Israelites into Canaan, the Jewish people inhabited their own land. It was Nebuchadnezzar, King of Babylon, who destroyed the First Temple, built by Solomon, and who exiled the Jews. The siege of Jerusalem began on the tenth of Tevet and the date has since been observed as a fast from dawn until dusk.

The fast is one of four which commemorate events connected with the fall of Jerusalem and the destruction of the Temple. The prophet Zachariah calls these (counting Nisan as the first month) "the fast of the fourth month, and the fast of the fifth, and the fast of the seventh, and the fast of the tenth..."

The seventeenth day of the fourth month, *shiva asar b'Tammuz,* marks the breaching of the walls of Jerusalem, which culminated in the destruction of the Second Temple by the Romans under Titus (Ta'anit 29). The fast of the fifth month is *Tisha b'Av,* the ninth of Av, commemorating the destruction of both the First Temple by Nebuchadnezzar in 586 BCE and the second Temple in 70 CE.

Tzom Gedaliah, the day after Rosh Hashana, was named after the murdered governor of the Jews appointed by Nebuchadnezzar; his assassination completed the *churban,* the national destruction of the First Commonwealth, and occurred on the third day of the seventh month.

The fast of the tenth month, *asarah b'Tevet* (the tenth of Tevet), rounds off those days marked in the Jewish calendar as periods of national mourning. Even at the peak of our happiness, we are told, Jerusalem and its every connotation is to be remembered: "... I will set Jerusalem above my highest joy" (Psalm 137). The fast is also known as *yom hakaddish haklali,* the day of the general kaddish, in remembrance of the victims of the Holocaust.

Their allegiance to the land of Israel gave the Jews a national identity even when they no longer had a country of their own. The prophecies of their eventual return and their unbroken link with the Hebrew language nurtured their hope throughout the centuries of dispersion.

While serving as expressions of sorrow at past events, the fasts also remind us of the sins of our ancestors that led to these tragedies. As the prophet Joel declares: "Sanctify ye a fast, call a solemn assembly, and cry unto the Lord. Rend your hearts and not your garments and turn [repent] unto the Lord your God."

They served, moreover, as opportunities for individual requests to the Almighty. The giving of charity is one way of making a fast day meaningful and of being worthy of God's response. As the Talmud states: "The merit of a fast day lies in the charity that is given during or immediately after the fast" (Berachot 6).

Other fast days, mainly of a private nature, are mentioned in the Talmud. They include *ta'anit chalom,* a fast observed after a bad dream (tractate Ta'anit 12), as well as the fast observed by some people on the yahrzeit of a parent (Orach Chayyim 568).

A fast of penitence is observed by a bride and bridegroom on the day of their marriage, reminding them of their obligations and privileges as they begin a new life together. This fast is broken immediately after the wedding ceremony (Even Ha'ezer 61).

The Talmud and rabbinic literature mention fasts which are sometimes observed in memory of outstanding personalities on the anniversaries of their death. These include Moses (Adar 7), Aaron (Av 1), Miriam (Nisan 10) and Joshua (Nisan 26).

Ta'anit Esther, the fast of Esther, precedes the festival of Purim and recalls Queen Esther's own fast before she sought an audience with Ahasuerus to plead for her people (Esther, 9:31).

The only fasts which are observed from sunset to sundown are Yom Kippur and Tisha b'Av. The former is

unique in that it is never postponed, even if it coincides with Shabbat. Most others would, in such circumstances, take place on Sunday, apart from the fast of Esther and the fast of the first-born, which are both then observed on the previous Thursday.

Additional penitential prayers are recited on fast days and special Torah readings are included in the services, which refer to the *zechut,* the merit, of the Patriarchs.

The Torah reading for most fasts is taken from Exodus, recording the story of Moses' intercession with God on behalf of the people who had sinned in worshipping the Golden Calf, and concluding with the Divine promise of forgiveness. The haftara, from Isaiah, calls on the exiles to seek God, who will deliver the people from captivity.

The book of Zechariah (8:19) suggests that all fasts "... shall be to the House of Judah joy and gladness, and cheerful seasons; therefore truth and peace shall ye love." Following the paths of truth and peace can avert the tragedies of a person and a people.

Purim (Feast of Lots)

THE READING of Megilat Esther on Purim is one of the four mitzvot authorised by the Sanhedrin and prophets for this minor festival. The other three are festivity and rejoicing, gifts to the poor and the mutual sending of gifts.

The festivity and rejoicing should include a family dinner, *seudah*; the gifts or charity should be given to at least two poor people; and the gifts to friends (*mishloach manot*) should consist of a minimum of two items of fruit, cakes, confectionery or drinks.

Most prominent of the features in the observance of this joyous day is the reading of the Megila both evening and morning. The sages made this decision during the time of Ezra, quoting as the source for their ruling Psalm 30, which states, "Forever will I give thanks to you."

The Megila is a book of thanksgiving which encapsulates the word "forever" in a period of one day and it is thus incumbent on us to read it at least twice, once at night and again during the day.

Of such great importance was the public reading and listening of the Megila that the rabbis ruled that even a person whose full-time occupation was the study of the Torah had to stop everything for the sake of the scroll.

Men and women are equally obliged to listen to (or read) the Megila. Children should also be encouraged to fulfil this duty, although toddlers who would otherwise not be taken to the synagogue should not be introduced to it on Purim, rather through regular services, when respect can be instilled in the mind of the youngster.

Although written on parchment and in the same script as a Torah scroll, the manner of reading the Megila is different from that of the Torah. The Scroll of Esther mentions "because of all the words of this letter"; the Megila is therefore unrolled, folded to look like a letter and laid down flat on the desk.

To fulfil the duty of hearing the Megila it is essential for it to be read in Hebrew. The rabbis did not want its sanctity to be debased by being written in a mixture of languages and its *neginot* (musical notation related to the Hebrew words) would, in any event, fit no other language.

It is customary for the congregation to read aloud four passages known as "verses of redemption." The commentator Avudraham suggests that these are four high points in the narrative and, with their recitation by the entire congregation, attention and excitement are kept to a maximum.

The custom is also said to stop the children falling asleep, thereby making the story of the miracle have an even greater impact on them. All four verses relate to Mordechai's pertinacity in helping to bring about the miracle of Purim.

The special selection of Psalms, Hallel, normally recited on festivals (including Chanucah) and Rosh Chodesh is not said on Purim since the reading of the Megila is considered as the Hallel of the day. These "songs of praise," moreover, are recited only over miracles which took place in Eretz Yisrael (the events of Purim occurred at Shushan in Persia). The Talmud adds that even after the Purim incident the Jews remained in exile as servants of Ahasuerus.

The *Al Hanisim* prayer is included in the grace after meals and in the silent Amidah prayer. It thanks God for the redemption of our people and refers to Haman's plot and his eventual downfall.

In the Middle Ages artists began illuminating the Scroll of Esther with illustrations of the Purim story or multicoloured geometric designs. Cases of gold, silver or wood were made to house the Megila, delicately engraved with appropriate designs.

When the First Temple was destroyed by Nebuchadnezzar in 586 BCE and the Jews were exiled, the prophet Jeremiah declared that God would bring the Jewish people back to their land after seventy years in exile (Jeremiah 29). During that period a number of kings ruled over the Persian and Babylonian empires.

Knowing of Jeremiah's prophecy, the monarchs were concerned to retain the Holy Land as part of their empire. Ahasuerus calculated that the period mentioned in the prophecy had ended by his reign and that God had not helped the Jewish people.

His calculation, however, was wrong, as explained in the Talmud (Megillah 11b). It was Darius, the son of Ahasuerus and of a Jewish mother, Esther, who, after his father's death, gave the order in 516 BCE to rebuild the Temple, exactly seventy years after the destruction of the First Temple, as foretold by Jeremiah.

Purim (Feast of Lots)

IN THE DAYS of the Messiah, when all the festivals will be forgotten and all the Books of the Prophets will lose their relevance, Purim will still be celebrated and the Book of Esther will still be studied.

It is not difficult to understand the reasoning behind this idea. Purim demonstrates to the Jew that he must put his entire trust in Divine Providence, and the Megila tells us how Amalek and all he stands for must be obliterated. These two situations can be fully appreciated only in the Messianic era.

The Sefer Hatoda'ah states that Purim is on a higher level than Yom Kippur; in rabbinic literature the term is *Yom Ha'kipurim*, a day *ke-purim*, "like Purim," since both days are designed to bring the Jew closer to God — albeit one by feasting and the other by fasting.

When Adar 14 occurs on a Friday and, unlike most other years, the special feast, *seudah*, must be eaten in the morning in order not to interfere with the preparations for Shabbat. The sending of gifts *(mishloach manot)* to friends and to the poor must be carried out as early as possible in the day.

The *brit mila* of a child due to be circumcised on Purim should be performed before the reading of the Megila in the morning. The commentary Darkei Moshe (693) states that since the Scroll of Esther contains the verse, *layehudim ha'yeta ora, v'simcha, v'sason, viy'kar* ("The Jews had light and joy and gladness and honour"), the infant being initiated into the ranks of the Jewish people should be eligible for that portion of joy to which he is entitled.

The reason why, in a leap year, the celebration of Purim is deferred until the second month of Adar is given by the Maharil (Rabbi Jacob ben Moses Moellin, 1360-1427), who suggests that the commemoration of our deliverance from the hands of Haman must occur as close as possible to Passover, the season when we celebrate Jewish deliverance from Egyptian slavery.

Throughout Jewish history in different parts of the world special Purims were fixed to commemorate deliverance from danger which threatened a whole community or family. Special megilot were written and read giving accounts of the events, prayers were recited and the days assumed the atmosphere of a semi-festival.

Purim Frankfurt was observed on Adar 20 to record the rescue of Frankfurt Jewry in 1616; Kislev 4 marked the institution of Purim Tiberias 200 years ago to celebrate the deliverance from an attack on the city by the ruler of Damascus. Another Purim (Shevat 17) commemorated a similar deliverance by the Jews of Saragossa in the seventeenth century.

An example of brevity in prayer is given in the *Al Hanisim* paragraph mentioned elsewhere. The full story of Purim is contained in this summary of 52 words, which includes all the highlights of the story mentioned in the Book of Esther's five chapters and 167 verses.

A well-known precept requires one to drink so much on Purim as not to be able to tell the difference in meaning between *arur Haman* (cursed is Haman) and *baruch Mordechai* (blessed is Mordechai). Coincidentally, the *gematria* (numerical value) of the letters of each phrase add up to the same total — 502.

Purim stories are numerous, jest and jollity being the order of the day. One incident relates to the well-known city of Chelm, famed for its simple-minded folk, where an annual get-together was traditionally held on this notable day in the Jewish calendar.

The wife of the shammas (beadle) was told to prepare a large barrel of wine months before Purim. When the barrel was full, she let it remain in the cellar of her house.

Just before Purim she decided to check on the state of the wine and, to her horror, found the barrel half-empty. She called her husband, who was shocked and perplexed at what had happened.

Both of them looked at all sides of the barrel and, after a while, the shammas' wife discovered a hole at the bottom. She told her husband that that must have been the way the wine had leaked from the vat.

Looking very wise, like all the people of Chelm, he exclaimed to his wife, "Don't be stupid! The hole doesn't explain the missing wine. Can't you see? The hole is at the bottom of the barrel and the wine is missing from the top!"

All the jesting and merrymaking aside, Purim reminds the Jew that he should maintain his trust in God, that truth prevails, and that the unity of the Jewish people brings salvation.

לַיְהוּדִים הָיְתָה אוֹרָה וְשִׂמְחָה וְשָׂשֹׂן וִיקָר.

Pesach (Passover)

MORE FUSS is made of the preparations for Pesach than for any other festive occasion in the Jewish calendar. The housewife turns her home upside-down to ensure that the religious requirement of having no chametz (leaven) in the house is strictly adhered to.

Alongside the positive commandment to eat matzo (unleavened bread) on Pesach as a reminder of the hasty exodus from Egypt are the negative commandments, "For seven days no leaven bread shall be found in your house" and "no leaven bread shall be seen by you." The whole purpose of the law is to impress on the Jew that pride, ostentation and pomposity — symbolised by chametz and its leavening agents, even to the smallest degree — are harmful to one's character, traits which are out of keeping with a Jewish way of life.

The same water, flour and heating process are used for the baking of chametz and matzo. Simply by our doing nothing and waiting, one becomes bread; the other, however, with constant and careful attention, becomes matzo. The rabbis use this to illustrate that inactivity leads to fermentation and to the sourness associated with it.

The Koretzer Rebbe was wont to quoting the Bible (II King 23) in support of the statement that no Passover was ever performed as it had been in the days of Josiah. This was because Josiah first burned all the altars and the pagan temples, thus cleansing them of chametz (metaphor for evil) completely. The Hebrew word "matzo" needs only a touch of the pen on the letter *hey* to make its components the same as those in "chametz" (albeit in different order).

Our sages learn another moral from the difference between normal bread, chametz — which differs in appearance and colour internally and externally — and matzo, which looks the same from all sides. This, they suggest, indicates that matzo reminds us to harmonise our thoughts and speech.

The Shabbat before Pesach is known as *Shabbat Hagadol*, the Great (or Long) Sabbath. It is customary for the rabbi of the community to explain in the synagogue the laws, rituals and problems which are encountered on this festival. The Midrash relates that on the Shabbat before leading the Israelites out of Egypt, Moses delivered a discourse on the Passover laws.

When Pesach begins immediately after Sabbath, all the preparations for the festival will already be completed by Shabbat Hagadol, so the rabbi will give his traditional address to the congregation on the preceding Shabbat. In fact, as indicated elsewhere on this page, there are a number of departures from the normal course of events when Nisan 14 occurs on a Shabbat.

Then the Fast of the Firstborn takes place on Thursday (Nisan 12), when it is customary for first-born males to attend a *siyum* — completion of a tractate of Talmud — in the synagogue. This calls for a celebration among all those present, thereby allowing the first-born to participate in the event and obviating the need to observe the fast.

Traditionally, the search for leaven *(bedikat chametz)* takes place immediately after nightfall on the same day, and the burning of the leaven *(biur chametz)* will be carried out on Friday morning. It is customary to place ten pieces of bread in different parts of the house, alluding to the story of Purim, when, on Nisan 13, Haman's ten sons wrote the decree to kill the Jews. The ten pieces of chametz are burned (normally on Nisan 14) to symbolise the failure of the plot against the Jews.

The real significance of the search and the burning of the chametz, says the "Ta'amei Haminhagim," is to serve as a visual-aid, impressing on the Jew the importance of removing the spiritual chametz, the evil inclination, from the heart and to destroy the imperfections within us.

Abudraham asks and answers the question why one does not recite the customary *shehecheyanu* prayer when carrying out a religious precept (in this case, searching for the chametz) for the first time in a year. One is sorry, he says, at having to destroy leavened items, and that particular prayer is said only on joyous occasions.

To ensure that every Jew is provided with the means to celebrate Pesach in the proper manner, many congregations have a fund known as the *maot chittin,* "money for matzo wheat," which allows for the distribution of matzot, wine and other Passover requirements to the needy.

The Bible calls the first day of the festival *Pesach* to denote that on that day the paschal lamb was sacrificed; the other days are known as *chag hamatzot* (Exodus 12). Both names are found throughout the Bible and the Pesach is referred to by most of the prophets as the festival commemorating Israel's journey to its homeland.

The Mishna speaks of *Pesach Mitzrayim,* the Passover of Egypt, and *Pesach l'dorot,* the Passover of the Generations (Pesachim 9). The former recalls the miracle that happened in Egypt on the night of the Exodus, while the latter refers to the festival observed by the Israelites immediately after their departure from Egypt, lasting until Nisan 21 (Exodus 12:18).

Pesach inspires hope not only for the Jewish people, but for all mankind. As *chag ha'aviv,* the Festival of Spring, it proclaims a message of aid to the oppressed, symbolising faith, freedom and salvation.

בְּדִיקַת חָמֵץ

Pesach (Passover)

AS THE JEWS left Egypt, they sang *(Shirat Hayam)* "This is my God and I will glorify him" (Exodus 15). Our sages tell us that this was a pledge to perform all the commandments, the mitzvot, in as glorious a manner as possible.

Certainly with regard to Pesach, artists, scribes, printers and silversmiths throughout the ages have been able to glorify the Seder table with ingenious designs, paintings and motifs: kiddush cups with chased biblical scenes; seder plates with engraved texts; embroidered matzo covers; illuminated Hagadot with numerous commentaries written by the greatest rabbis. Pesach indeed lends itself to the glorification of the mitzva and to the creation of a joyous event.

Yet in its narrative of the Exodus the Torah mentions neither joy nor happiness, nor does it record the miracle of the defeat of the Egyptians; it speaks only of the salvation of the Jews. Pesach is celebrated because of Israel's freedom and not because of Egypt's punishment.

The fact is that we never exult over the defeat of our enemies. This is illustrated by the recitation of the Ten Plagues during the seder service when, after mention of each of the plagues, a drop of wine is spilled from the full cup to signify incomplete happiness caused by the downfall of our foes, who are yet human beings.

Because there is no future for the Jewish people without its children, Pesach in particular is centred on the younger generation. From the opening of the seder service, with the singing by the youngest child of the Ma Nishtana, to the catchy songs at the end of the Hagada, there are constant questions and answers, customs and rituals which make the child wonder and ask why this night is indeed so different and special.

Even the fact that the children are encouraged to stay up late — a treat at the best of times — singles out the seder night, when we make sure that the youngsters are still wide enough awake to "steal" the Afikoman (the last food eaten at the seder) and to receive the promise of a prize on its return to the festive table.

Numbers play an important role during Pesach, especially at the seder: the *three* matzot, *four* cups of wine, *fifteen* ceremonies listed in the order of service, the same number of thanks to God in the Dayeinu song, and the *four hundred* years of slavery foretold to Abraham by God.

The Maharal of Prague, Judah Loew ben Bezalel (1525-1609), wrote that the three matzot represent the Patriarchs, Abraham, Isaac and Jacob, without whom there would be no Jewish nation, and certainly no miracle of freedom for the Jewish people. The four cups of wine, he added, are in honour of the Matriarchs, Sarah, Rebecca, Leah and Rachel, without whose righteousness and merit the redemption of Israel would not have occurred.

Many hundreds of melodies have been composed for the seder, with many more handed down from father to son and from generation to generation. Ashkenazi and Sephardi tunes have been liberally intermingled and in the field of Pesach music modern Israel has broken down the cultural barriers.

Thus Pesach truly illustrates the meaning of *am kadosh*, a holy people, when all sections of the community demonstrate *en famille* that Jewish living can best be experienced through freedom, gratitude to God and observance of the mitzvot.

It is customary for the head of the household, who conducts the seder service, to wear a white robe, a *kittel*, which serves both as a sign of purity and as a visible reminder to be humble despite the Hagada story of Israel's victory. The celebrant conducting the sacred seder is compared to the High Priest who was clothed in white while performing the *Avodah* service in the Holy of Holies of the Temple.

The famous scholar and Cabalist, Rabbi Yeshayah Horowitz (known as the Shelah), who died in Tiberias in 1630, wrote: "On returning home after the evening service, one should conduct oneself as a prince. There should be an abundance of silver and gold, together with garments of silk and tapestry, to demonstrate to all on this seder night how one's heart rejoices at the great kindness of God.

"This night, and all the laws connected with it, are of the utmost holiness, for it was on this night that God chose us to be His people and sanctified us with His commandments. It is therefore unseemly for anyone to indulge in idle talk on this great night, so that the bond between each Jew and the Almighty should not be broken.

"Everyone should devote himself solely to the mitzvot of the night, to telling of the miracles of the Exodus and to teaching them to the members of his household."

The Talmud (Pesachim 116) states that the mitzva of relating the Exodus story, which is mentioned four times in the Torah, is fulfilled by "beginning with shame and ending with praise": from idol worship and slavery to liberation, receiving the Torah and entry into Eretz Yisrael.

Yom Ha'atzmaut (Israel Independence Day)

ON IYAR 5, 5708 (May 14, 1948), at precisely four in the afternoon on the eve of Shabbat, David Ben-Gurion picked up a parchment scroll and declared: "In the Land of Israel the Jewish people came into being. In this land was shaped their spiritual, religious and national character.

"Here they created a culture of national and universal import and gave to the world the eternal Book of Books. . . . With trust in the Almighty, we set our hand to this declaration at this session of the Provisional Council of State . . . in the city of Tel Aviv."

An elderly rabbi present, overcome with emotion, recited aloud the thanksgiving blessing, *Shehecheyanu*. Then, one by one, the leaders in the room added their signatures to the scroll of the establishment of the State of Israel. The whole ceremony took barely half an hour.

Yom Ha'atzmaut (Independence Day) is now a natural part of the Jewish calendar. It is a new holiday which has its origin, for the first time since Chanucah, in Israel itself.

The former Chief Rabbi of Jerusalem, Rabbi Zvi Pesach Frank (in his foreword to "Army Law in Israel," 1949), and the late Gaon, Rabbi Meshullam Rath (Responsa, Kol Mevaser, 21), are just two of the halachic authorities living at the time of Israel's rebirth who wrote about the miracle of the great deliverance and the institution of a festive day to commemorate it.

God described the land to the Patriarchs as being a heritage to their seed. Much later, in the era of the prophets, all major prophetical pronouncements referred to the importance of Zion and the ingathering of the exiles.

Throughout history we have referred to Zion and to the Holy Land in our prayers, our rituals and our observances. The link between the people and the land of Israel has never been broken.

Just as the Fast of Esther is linked to Purim, so is Yom Hazikaron (Memorial Day) connected to Yom Ha'atzmaut. Starting at sundown, it remembers and honours those who made the supreme sacrifice in the

defence of Israel and her people.

The sound of sirens heralds a two-minute silence, during which all Israel pauses to reflect of the heroism of the fallen, and the day concludes with yet more sirens signifying the start of Yom Ha'atzmaut and its celebrations.

During the early months of 1949 a decision was made with regard to the official emblem of the new State. On the question of Israel's flag there was no dispute, since the blue and white flag, taken from the colours of the tallit (prayer shawl), had already been used for some time.

The emblem, however, presented differences of opinion. Some maintained that for the people of the Book, a sefer Torah, or a Bible, or the tablets of the Ten Commandments, would be appropriate. Others suggested the Burning Bush unconsumed, representing Israel's indestructibility.

In the end it was agreed to adopt the seven-branched candelabrum made by Moses for use in the tabernacle (and later in the Temple), surrounded by two olive branches. The colours adopted were again blue and white.

Of the symbolism surrounding blue, Rabbi Samson Raphael Hirsch once declared: "The colour which, at the limit of our horizon, seems to point to a realm beyond human sight, representing the godliness which is revealed to us, the colour of God's bond with man, the sign of spirituality, of godliness, permeating and directing the whole life of a pure human being."

The emblem itself, the menorah, depicts light to the Jews and to humanity at large. The olive branches represent the oil used for the menorah.

The rabbis have compared the oil pressing process to the Jewish people through the ages: though they have gone through oppression, persecution and suffering, it was precisely at these periods that the best qualities and talents of our people emerged. Oil, similarly, always rises above other liquids and cannot itself be diluted.

Comparisons with the Jewish people and the Torah are self-evident. The sages deduce from the source of the commandment, "They shall bring thee pure olive oil beaten for the light, to cause the lamp to burn always" (Exodus 27), that the general community must always care for the religious education of its children.

This summarises the qualities for which Israel stands: to bring spiritual light to Jewry and to mankind; to spread education, science and culture; to highlight the true values of life as prescribed by the Torah.

This thought is best expressed in the words of the late Rishon le Zion, the Sephardi Chief Rabbi Benzion Uziel (1880-1953), who wrote of Israel's rebirth in his last will and testament:

"Remember this and ponder deeply over it. Know and believe that the hand of the Lord has done this in order to fulfil the message of the prophets for the eternal welfare of His people and that of the whole world, which depends on Israel's observance of the words of the Torah.

"Thus all the peoples will learn to know the unity of God and His faith, which will bring true peace in the world, where no man will do harm to his neighbour and the land will be full of knowledge as the waters cover the sea."

Lag B'omer

THE TWO semi-festivals in the Jewish calendar which are commonly known by a specific number and on which children enjoy outdoor activities are Lag b'Omer (the 33rd day of the period between Pesach and Shavuot) and Tu BiShvat (Shevat 15, the New Year for Trees).

The minor festival, Lag B'omer, is associated with a number of events which happened on the 33rd day of the Omer, which coincides with Iyar 18. Best known of these dates is the cessation of the plague which broke out among the 24,000 pupils of Rabbi Akiva in the second century. According to the Talmud, they were thus punished because they did not treat each other with respect and honour (Yevamot 62).

Another historical connection is the rebellion led by Bar Kochba, a contemporary of Rabbi Akiva, against the Romans in their fight for national independence. On that day they won a major victory.

Both events, the end of the plague and Bar Kochba's success, resulted in this date being observed as a break in the period of mourning when such celebrations as marriages and public entertainment are prohibited. Both the advent of the plague and the failure of the revolt had given rise to a period of national mourning and, since the fall of Betar in the year 135, Jews have kept alive the spirit of national independence by abstaining from any rejoicing during 33 of the 49 days between Pesach and Shavuot.

Festivities take place in Israel on Lag b'Omer at the hillside village of Meron, near Safed. This is the burial-place of the distinguished pupil of Rabbi Akiva and the reputed author of the Cabalistic Zohar, the saintly Rabbi Shimon bar Yochai, and his son, Rabbi Elazar. The two hid in a cave at Meron for 13 years after being sentenced to death by the Romans (Shabbat 33), having upheld the right of the Jews to study the Torah and to live in accordance with its teachings.

Thousands of people make a pilgrimage to this spot, where prayers are recited and bonfires are lit to the accompaniment of songs and dances

in praise of Shimon bar Yochai, who, according to tradition, died on this day.

The custom of cutting a boy's hair only after his third birthday is reserved for Lag b'Omer, the day when it is permissible to have a haircut during the Omer period. In Israel hundreds of little boys are among the pilgrims to Meron, where, on the side of hill near the tomb of bar Yochai, the haircutting ceremony is held in a dignified yet joyful manner.

The Talmud (Berachot 62) relates how a friend of Rabbi Akiva, Pappus ben Yehudah, asked him whether he was not afraid of teaching the Torah in view of the Roman decree forbidding it. Akiva replied: "I will answer you with a fable.

"A fox was once walking along a river bank and saw fish scurrying to and fro. 'From what are you fleeing?' he asked them. 'From the nets cast by the fishermen,' they replied.

"'Why not come up on to dry land, so that you and I can live together as our ancestors did?' 'You are said to be the cleverest of animals; how can you suggest such a thing?' they answered. 'If we are afraid in our natural surroundings, how much more so would we be on dry land, the element in which we would surely die?'

"So it is with us Jews," continued Rabbi Akiva. "If we are in danger when we sit and study the Torah, which is our life — 'For it is your life and the length of your days' (Deuteronomy 30:20) — how much more dangerous would our lives be without it?"

The Talmud notes (Kiddushin 72) that on the day Akiva died, the compiler and editor of the Mishna, Yehuda HaNasi, was born, to continue the unbroken chain of Torah tradition since Mount Sinai. Iyar 18 has also been given as the day the children of Israel first received manna in the wilderness after their exodus from Egypt.

The expression, Sefirat ha'Omer (the counting of the Omer), is taken from Leviticus 23:10, which states that a farmer was obliged to bring an offering (the *omer*, a measure equal to one-tenth of an *ephah*) of the first fruits of the barley harvest on "the morrow after the Sabbath" — which the rabbis took to mean the second day of Pesach — and to count seven full weeks until the new offering could be brought, which would be celebrated as the festival of Shavuot.

A blessing is said every night during this seven-week period. All kinds of aids have been devised to help one remember the exact date of the Omer, including ornamental wooden Omer counters, tables and wall calendars, to comply with the command, "And you shall count . . . seven complete weeks . . . 50 days" (Leviticus 23:15).

This period of seven weeks is said to link the two freedoms — the physical and the spiritual — of the Jewish people. At the time of the Exodus, on Pesach, they became a free people; when the received the Torah at Sinai, on Shavuot, they became a people with a religion.

Yom Yerushalayim (Jerusalem Day)

IT IS Wednesday, June 7, 1967, Iyar 28, 5727, 19 years and 23 days after the first Yom Ha'atzmaut. At 9.50 a.m. the Temple Mount is liberated and Jerusalem reunited. Twenty-five minutes later, the chief chaplain to the Israel Defence Forces, Rabbi Shlomo Goren, arrives in a jeep, carrying a sefer Torah, and blows the shofar at the Western Wall.

The Defence Minister, General Moshe Dayan, stands before the Wall, tears a piece of paper from his notebook and writes, ...*Shalom al Yisrael*, "Peace be upon Israel." He places it as a *kvittel*, a written plea, between the crevices of the old, huge stones of the Wall, observing an age-long Jewish tradition. General Itzhak Rabin does the same, having written, *Zeh hayom... nagilah v'nismechah vo*, "This is the day which the Lord hath made; we will be glad and rejoice thereon" (Psalms).

For the first time since the year 70, Jews are free to stand, pray and dance at the *kotel ma'aravi*, the Western Wall, the only remaining section of the holy Temple. It is the crowning

achievement of the Six-Day War.

The late head of the Ponevez Yeshiva in Bnei Brak, Rabbi Yosef Kahaneman, wrote six years after this great event: "Our sages said that 'the recipient of divine grace does not himself recognise the miracle.' Even those who with their own eyes saw wonders and experienced the miraculous deliverance in the wars of Israel, in Jerusalem and the site of the Holy Temple, fail to express properly the depth of their feelings. We must look upon this as a preamble to the final redemption."

Everyone who lived through that period of the "shadow of death" breathed a sigh of relief when, on the third day of the war, came the historic announcement, "All of Jerusalem is in our hands," followed by the sounding of the shofar and the singing of Psalms and the Hatikvah by the first soldiers to arrive at the Wall. Here the religious and the irreligious together shed tears of joy.

Yom Yerushalayim is commemorated as a day of thanksgiving, with a special ceremony at the Western Wall attended by tens of thousands, who watch the kindling of flames in memory of those who died in the battle of liberation.

With the barriers down and Jerusalem now united, those who wish to do so can fulfil the injunction in Psalm 48, "Walk about Zion and go round about her; count the towers thereof."

Throughout the centuries Jews have been reminded of Zion and Jerusalem through prayers and supplications recited daily and through numerous actions which allude to the centrality of Jerusalem in Jewish life.

The Talmud states: "A Jew outside the Land of Israel wishing to pray turns his heart towards the Land of Israel; if he is in the Land, he turns his heart towards Jerusalem; if he is in Jerusalem, he turns his heart towards the Holy of Holies; if he is in the Holy of Holies, he turns his heart towards the cover of the Holy Ark. Thus, all Jews praying direct their hearts towards one place" (Berachot 30).

It is remarkable, even miraculous, how the Western Wall has been able to

withstand more than a dozen wars fought in and for Jerusalem. This magnetic piece of architecture, which is neither aesthetic nor picturesque, attracts every type of Jew to its stones for prayer, thought and meditation. To every Jew it symbolises the indestructibility of the Jewish people.

A legend is told that when the Temple was being built, the work was divided among the various sections of the population. The building of the Western Wall became the responsibility of the poor, and they worked hard to construct it, since they were unable to afford labourers to do their work for them. When the Temple was destroyed, the Angels descended from heaven and spread their wings, saying: "This wall, the work of the poor, shall never be destroyed."

Four thousand years ago, when Abraham came to Jerusalem, it was called Salem. During the period of the Judges it was known as Jebus, and after that it was given the Hebrew name *Yerushalayim*, from the word *ir* (city) and *shalom* (peace). Jerusalem, the City of Peace, also became known as the Holy City through the building of the First Temple by King Solomon.

Yom Yerushalayim deserves its rightful place in the calendar, with proper Yomtov celebrations of thanksgiving and rejoicing, of song and praise, in recognition of the miraculous events which have taken place in our own days and before our own eyes. We owe it to our children and grandchildren to fix this day firmly as a great and historic event and to celebrate it in a fitting manner.

Shavuot (Pentecost)

THE COUNTING of days is specified for various occasions in the Torah. Maimonides compares the counting of the Omer between Pesach and Shavuot to the counting of weeks and days before an exciting and important event.

The Exodus was of great significance on its own account, with the Jewish people becoming physically free; of equal magnitude, however, and linked to it, was the spiritual freedom they attained by their acceptance of the Torah at Mount Sinai on Shavuot.

This festival is commonly known as *Z'man matan torateinu*, the anniversary (or season) of the Giving of the Law, the name used in the Amidah and the Kiddush. But the Torah uses three other names for this, the second of the *shalosh regalim* (pilgrim festivals): *chag habikkurim*, the Festival of the First Fruits; *chag hakatzir*, the Feast of the Harvest; and *chag hashavuot*, the Festival of Weeks.

Later, the rabbis added the name *atzeret*, "concluding" the complete redemption which began on Pesach. They felt it was wrong to limit the celebrations for the Giving of the Law to just one or two days, since every day had to be considered as a new acceptance of the Torah and its mitzvot.

It is customary on Shavuot to decorate both synagogue and home with greenery and flowers, to remind one of the harvest nature of the event. The foliage is also meant to serve as a reminder of the leading figure in this momentous happening — Moses — whose discovery and rescue among the reeds of the Nile led to the Divine Revelation at Sinai.

Similarly, the floral decorations symbolise the verdant oasis that lay at the foot of the mountain, where the flocks grazed (Otzar Yisrael, Volume 10), while at the same time the branches and leaves remind us that the Torah is referred to as the "Tree of Life."

As if in anticipation of the great event, it has long been customary to stay up on Shavuot eve for a reading of an anthology of sacred literature known as *Tikkun Leil Shavuot*, and also to take part in lectures and discussions on relevant themes. During the night traditional refreshments are served, including honey and cheese cake, as well as blintzes and other dairy foods, since the Torah and the Land of Israel are compared to the nourishing nature of both milk and honey (Song of Songs 4; Exodus 3, etc.).

In Yemen, the Sephardi Jews used to spend the night studying the "Sefer Hamitzvot" of Maimonides.

At dawn the usual festival morning services are held, including an eleventh-century Aramaic poem, "Akdamot," which is chanted before the reading of the Law. It describes the angels' praises of God and speaks of the Jewish people's attachment to the Almighty and His Torah, thanking Him for the gift of the Law. The poem, which is written in a double alphabetical acrostic, has plaintive chant which was composed in London in 1870 (Otzar Yisrael, Volume 2).

A custom dating back to talmudic times is the public reading of the Book of Ruth. It was on Shavuot that Ruth accepted the Torah and its teachings, and on Shavuot we, too, accept the Torah anew as our guide in our journey through life. Ruth lived to see her great-grandson David become king; he was born on Shavuot and died on that day, 70 years later. Some read

the entire Book of Psalms on the festival to commemorate these events.

The fourteenth-century Rabbeinu Bachya stated that all the mitzvot in the Torah could be divided into three categories. Quoting the verse, "But the thing is very near to you, in your mouth and in your heart, that you may do it" (Deuteronomy 30), he explained this to mean that one's mouth, heart and actions are the agents for fulfilling the commandments: by study and speech; by belief and faith; by observance and kind deeds.

The total number of positive and negative commandments in the Torah is 613, known in Hebrew as *taryag* (the equivalent numerical value). The Talmud states: "The 248 positive commandments correspond to the number of organs in the human body, as if every part of the body wishes to perform a mitzva. The 365 negative commandments correspond to the number of days in a solar year, as if every 'day' wishes that no transgression should be committed thereon" (Makkot 23).

Maimonides cites this as proof that the sum of 613 (mitzvot) will never be diminished. Rabbeinu Bachya agrees with this view, quoting the verse in Deuteronomy 33 which refers to the Torah as "an inheritance of the congregation of Israel," and the same expression in Exodus 6, which speaks of the Land of Israel as "an inheritance." Both the Torah and the Land are "an inheritance," eternal and unbroken.

The main purpose of Shavuot is to stress the fact that the Torah should serve as a guide for every Jew.

The 'Three Weeks'

THE PERIOD in the Jewish calendar known as the three weeks, commemorating historical events of national grief, starts with the fast day of the seventeenth of Tammuz and ends with the fast of the ninth of Av (Tisha b'Av).

These twenty-one days are called in Hebrew *yem'ei bein hametzarim*, "the days of difficult straits" or "the days between the fences" (Lamentations 1:3). All forms of rejoicing are limited during this period of semi-mourning, with the intensity of customs increasing daily, until they reach their peak on Tisha b'Av, when full mourning regulations are observed.

Although weddings are not permitted during this period, engagement celebrations and the feasts for a brit or a pidyan haben may take place, but without the accompaniment of music.

It is customary not to eat new fruit or to wear a new garment during the three weeks, thus avoiding the need to recite the special *shehecheyanu* blessing, since this is a period of calamity. But this does not apply to those mitzvot (such as the two cited above) which occur within a set time or to the recitation of *shehecheyanu* on Shabbat, when mourning of any kind is not allowed. Moreover, a sick person or a pregnant woman who is advised to eat a new fruit may do so and recite the *shehecheyanu* blessing.

On Tammuz 17 five tragedies are said to have taken place. The first was when Moses, on his descent from Mount Sinai, saw the Israelites worshipping the Golden Calf and smashed the Tablets of the Law (Exodus 32).

The daily offering *(tamid)* was suspended in the First Temple on Tammuz 17 owing to the scarcity of cattle during the siege; a sefer Torah was burned by the Syrian general, Apostomos, an officer of Antiochus; a heathen idol was placed in the Temple compound; and Titus breached the walls of Jerusalem, thus precipitating the destruction of the Second Temple.

The Talmud states that in the case of the First Temple, the breach was made in the city on the ninth of Tammuz, but that in the case of the Second Temple, it occurred on the seventeenth. Since the loss of the Second Temple was a more severe blow, the fast was fixed for the seventeenth (Ta'anit 29). To have had two fast days within close proximity to each other was regarded by the rabbis as being too excessive a burden on the community.

Most sad days in the Jewish calendar are connected with the destruction of the Temple (the *bet hamikdash*). Fast days were instituted to instil into our people the importance of the pledge made by the exiles alongside the rivers of Babylon, "If I forget thee, O Jerusalem, may my right hand lose its cunning. Let my tongue cleave to the roof of my mouth if I remember thee not, if I set not Jerusalem above my chiefest joy" (Psalm 137).

Many ask why we should continue to observe these fast days when, after so many centuries, we once again have our own land. One answer was given by the then commander-in-chief of the Israel Defence Forces, Itzhak Rabin, after the Six-Day War of 1967: "Although we have been victorious in the Six-Day War, we have not yet arrived at the Seventh Day of rest and peace."

The fast days decreed by the prophets and sages were designed to enable the Jews to recall the misdeeds of their forefathers which led to national calamities, thereby reviewing their own actions, changing those ways which need improving, and making them worthy of God's mercy and redemption.

"Sanctify ye a fast, call a solemn assembly, gather all the elders and all the inhabitants of the land to the house of the Lord your God and cry unto the Lord" (Joel 1:14). The essential significance of the fast is the consequential act of repentance.

The Chasidic Rebbe of Sassov once said: "If your neighbour offends you, refrain from wrath, and it will be more pleasing in the sight of God than a thousand fast days." And another scholar observed: "It is more desirable to abstain from idle talk than to abstain from eating, since this will injure neither the body nor the soul." Nevertheless, fast days have been ordained by prophetic decree and throughout the generations they have existed to arouse the conscience of our people.

The four fast days centred on the loss of Israel's past glory and independence are observed on the third of Tishri (Tzom Gedalia), the tenth of Tevet (Asarah b'Tevet), the seventeenth of Tammuz and the ninth of Av. All but the last are observed from daybreak to nightfall, whereas Tisha b'Av, like Yom Kippur, begins at sunset and ends the following night.

A number of special prayers are inserted into sections of the morning and afternoon services, together with Torah readings in which Moses pleads with God to remember the Covenant He made with the Patriachs and to forgive the Israelites for worshipping the Golden Calf (Exodus 32 and 34).

The afternoon service includes a haftara from Isaiah which opens with the injunction, "Seek ye the Lord while He may be found." The prophet pleads with the people, "Let the wicked forsake his way, and the unrighteous man his thoughts, and let him return to the Lord."

יְמֵי בֵּין הַמְּצָרִים

Tishah B'Av (9th of Av)/Holocaust Day

WHILE THE Israelites were in the wilderness, the spies brought back a slanderous report on the Promised Land. The people lost faith and wept. It was the eve of the ninth of Av.

Centuries later, both the first and the second Temple were destroyed on the same date. "Because you had no cause to weep, when the spies gave a false report about Canaan, this day will remain a day for weeping for generations to come" (Talmud; Ta'anit 29).

Other national calamities occurred on this day, including the fall of Bar Kochba's fortress at Betar in the year 135 and the expulsion of the Jews from Spain in 1492. In 1290 King Edward's decree expelling the Jews from Britain was written on that day.

As a fast day Tisha b'Av resembles Yom Kippur in that the restrictions are observed from sundown to sunset. If, however, it falls on a Sabbath it is postponed until the following day, whereas Yom Kippur, the "Sabbath of Sabbaths," is never put off.

This saddest and most tragic date in the Jewish calendar still has

significance in contemporary Jewish life, both as a reminder of the destruction of the religious centre of our people and as an opportunity to mourn the many occasions in our history — culminating in the twentieth-century Holocaust — when our lives were filled with suffering and sorrow.

The prelude to Tisha b'Av is Shabbat Chazon, the Sabbath of the Vision, which takes its name from the first words of Isaiah, the haftara for that day, chanted to the same mournful melody used to recite the Book of Lamentations on Tisha b'Av.

When Shabbat Chazon falls on the eve of the fast, havdala is not recited until after the fast, when a shortened form is said.

On the evening of Tisha b'Av, the Book of Lamentations *(Eichah)* is read. In five chapters the prophet Jeremiah, who witnessed the last days of the first Temple, expresses his heartbreaking lament over the destruction and desolation of Jerusalem.

After the normal morning service, a collection of liturgical dirges is read. Written by some of the greatest poets — including Ibn Gabirol and Yehuda Halevi — these *kinot* record events of Jewish suffering and describe how the martyrs died sanctifying God's name and His teachings. The synagogue exudes sadness and mourning, with the Ark curtain and the decorative cover of the reader's desk removed to intensify the atmosphere.

The story is told of how the Emperor Napoleon, passing a Paris synagogue on Tisha b'Av, noticed Jews sitting on the ground, lamenting the destruction of the Temple and the land as if the calamity had only just happened. He said to his companions: "This people is destined for a successful future in its own land. Which other people has mourned and hoped for thousands of years?"

The talit and tefilin are not worn as on a normal morning service, since they are "religious adornments," symbols of beauty. Instead, they are donned during the mincha (afternoon) service. Curiously, on this

day of national mourning, the special prayer of supplication, *tachanun*, is omitted. The Talmud and Midrash explain this anomaly by quoting the verse in Lamentations (1,15.) which classifies the day of our national disaster as *moed*, a festival.

As throughout Jewish history, when the hour seemed bleakest, encouragement and comfort suddenly emerged to give renewed strength and optimism for the future, so that immediately after Tisha b'Av we enter the seven weeks of comfort, *shiva d'nechemta*. On each Shabbat, starting with Isaiah's fortieth chapter — "Comfort ye, comfort ye, my people, saith your God" — messages of consolation and the promise of eventual redemption are read.

On the first Sabbath, known as Shabat Nachamu (from the opening word of the haftara), the Torah reading includes the Ten Commandments and the Shema, bringing joy to the Sabbath which follows the three weeks of sadness. The commentator Abudraham attempts to link the seven haftarot of consolation in sequence, concluding with Israel being fully comforted by the divine promise of deliverance.

Commenting on the talmudic saying, "had Israel properly observed only two Sabbaths, they could have been redeemed immediately" (Shabbat 118), the Chasidic rabbi of Vitebsk, Rabbi Menachem Mendel, said that this applied to Shabbat Chazon and Shabbat Nachamu, which depict hope and salvation even in the throes of disaster.

Another sad day in the Jewish calendar is Holocaust Memorial Day, *Yom Hashoa*, observed on the Hebrew day of the twenty-eighth of Nisan in memory of the six million Jews killed in Europe during the Nazi era. In Israel it is a day of mourning; sirens are sounded in the morning, when a two-minute silence brings everything to a standstill as a mark of respect in memory of those who died in that tragic period. Most of the survivors rebuilt their lives in the re-established State of Israel dedicated to ensuring that such an evil will never happen again.

Ellul

DURING THE month of Ellul the Jew is given every opportunity adequately to prepare for the High Holy-days, the most awesome occasion in the Jewish calendar. From the first of Ellul, the sound of the shofar can be heard at the end of every weekday morning service.

Maimonides tells us that the sound of the shofar beckons us to a period of introspection. "Awake you sleepers from your slumber and you drowsy ones from your napping; search your ways and repent."

The hollowed-out horn of the sheep, goat, gazelle or antelope may be used for a shofar; because of its association with the idolatry of the Golden Calf, however, the horn of a cow is not permissible (Mishna, Rosh Hashana 3).

Nor may the shofar be embellished with gold, silver or any other ornaments, though the exterior may be carved with geometric shapes or inscriptions dealing with the shofar.

The one Ellul weekday on which the shofar is not sounded is the day before Rosh Hashana (unless it is Friday). This highlights the distinction between the month-long blowing, which is "voluntary" and based on a rabbinic ruling, and that of Rosh Hashana, which is "obligatory," having been specifically commanded in Leviticus 23 and Numbers 29.

Of all the musical instruments used in the sacred service of the Temple, the shofar alone has survived. During the Babylonian captivity, after the destruction of the First Temple, the Jews lived as a compact religious and cultural group. They were thus able to preserve their spiritual life, which included the making of music and maintaining their musical tradition.

A different situation prevailed, however, after the fall of the Second Temple in the year 70. The Jews were dispersed throughout the known world, no longer able to maintain an homogeneous musical culture.

All the efforts of the rabbis were concentrated on the religious and spiritual survival of the Jewish people, not on saving the musical instruments used in the Temple. In any case, the rabbis had ruled that, as a sign of

mourning over the destruction of the Temple, music was forbidden.

Thereafter, the ancient musical heritage of the Jewish people was lost, leaving only a primitive instrument of religious importance — the shofar.

The Talmud (Rosh Hashana 27) goes into great detail over the shofar's manufacture, repair, size and use, together with its validity for religious purposes. The prophet Amos declares that its main purpose is for the hearer to be stirred by its shrill sounds, to take stock spiritually and to be moved to repent: "If a shofar is blown in the city, shall the people not tremble?"

The shofar was first heard at the giving of the Torah on Mount Sinai (Exodus 19) and it was constantly used to herald the approach of the Sabbath, the new moon and the festivals. It was also blown to proclaim the Jubilee Year (Leviticus 25), to summon the people to war, and to denote special fast days in times of drought or disaster.

Ellul serves to remind the Jew of Moses' second ascent on Mount Sinai after the sin of the Golden Calf. The shofar was heard so that the Israelites might not again err in their ways.

Moses ascended the mountain in the early morning of Rosh Chodesh Ellul and stayed there until the tenth of Tishri, Yom Kippur, when he brought down the second tablets. These 40 days have throughout the generations served as a period of reflection, repentance and forgiveness.

The person assigned the task of blowing the shofar (the *ba'al tekiah*) should be both competent and pious. The story is told of the Berditschever Rebbe who, wishing to engage a *ba'al tekiah*, asked each of the applicants what special caba- listic thoughts he had in mind during the shofar-blowing. None of the ans- wers given to the would-be shofar blowers satisfied him.

One man told him, however: "I am not learned and I have no mystical thoughts. But I have four daughters of marriage- able age and have little money for their dowries. When I blow the shofar, I think: 'Lord of the Universe, I have performed my duty in carrying out thy command; do Thou also Thy duty and send me worthy partners for my dear daughters'." The rabbi immediately appointed him to blow the shofar.

The rabbis interpreted the word Ellul as an abbreviation for the initial letters of the words composed by Solomon (Song of Songs 6:3), *ani l'dodi v'dodi li*, "I belong to my friend and my friend is mine," indicating that during Ellul, before the High Holy- days, "my friend (God) and I are close to each other."

The four words, moreover, all end with the letter *yod*, whose numerical value is ten; the total of 40 is another reminder of the 40 days from the first of Ellul to Yom Kippur.

It is customary during Ellul to send blessings and greetings for the New Year when corresponding with family and friends. The graves of departed relatives are visited during this month as a sign of respect and to reflect on the meaning of the approaching season as a period of self-examination, when one sets a high standard of life and establishes an appropriate state of holiness.

Why, on the last Shabbat of Ellul, do we not announce the incoming month (Tishri), as is the custom for all other months? The Talmud (Rosh Hashana 8) says that this is in order to confuse the adversary (Satan) by keeping the date of the Day of Judgement "concealed" or "secret."

61

Repentance

REPENTANCE, states the Talmud, was one of the seven concepts created before the world came into being (Pesachim 54). Having granted man free will, God realised that by nature a person was likely at times to digress from the ways of the Torah.

"For there is not a righteous man on earth who does (only) good and does not sin," says Ecclesiastes. To err is human, so the Almighty has given us an opportunity to repent — *teshuva*, from the Hebrew root, "to return."

This act of penitence is one of the positive commandments: "And you shall return to the Lord your God and shall obey His voice" (Deuteronomy 30). This is linked with the ingathering of the exiles, which the late Chief Rabbi Kook of Palestine interpreted as being a form of national repentance in the messianic era.

Much is heard today about the *ba'al teshuva* and *chozer bitshuva* movements, where those wishing to find their spiritual and religious roots "return" to the paths of the Jew, based on faith and observance as ordained in the Torah. Many colleges have been established in Israel and elsewhere in the Jewish world to cater for such penitents.

Says Isaiah: "Seek the Lord while he can be found; call on Him while He is near. Let the wicked forsake his way, and the man of iniquity his thoughts; and let him return to the Eternal and He will have compassion on Him, and to our God, for He will abundantly pardon."

These are the days most suitable for heavenly forgiveness, when God is more accessible to those who have lost their way and when His hand is outstretched to receive those who seek Him. As the prophet Amos declared: "For the Eternal says this to the House of Israel: 'Seek Me and you shall live'."

The act of repentance requires every Jew to re-evaluate his outlook on life, to redefine its values and priorities. This is attained by a threefold process: confession (*viddui*), acknowledgement of one's transgressions (*hakarat hatchet*), and resolution (*kabala l'haba*).

The act of repentance is brought

Repentance – between man and God; between man and his neighbour

home every weekday during the recitation of the Amida, the fifth benediction of which implores the Almighty to "bring us back in perfect repentance unto Thy presence." Thus we learn that every day, and not merely the Days of Awe, require us to repent.

The rabbis, in fact, advised that one should "repent one day before your death" (Avot 2). Since that day cannot be determined, a person should examine his actions every day (Avot d'Rabbi Natan 15).

Rabeinu Bachya, in his "Duties of the Heart," states that the root of repentance is humility. "It was by Divine grace that man was given the capacity to correct his errors and by means of repentance to regain the service of God that he had lost."

One who has become ill through a faulty diet can regain his health only by correcting that diet, avoiding those foods which have been harmful. Similarly, the Torah and the mitzvot are the correct nourishment for the well-being of the soul.

The Chasidic Gerer Rebbe explained the prayer, "And sweeten, O Lord, the words of Thy Torah in our mouth," as meaning that the drink which is sweet to a person in good health is bitter to one who is sick. "In the same way," he commented, "the healthy mind appreciates the Torah which the morbid mind dislikes.

"We therefore petition the Lord to help us to rid ourselves of all sin through repentance. Then will God's word be sweet to our mind, cleansed and purified."

It is during Ellul that this intensive spiritual and moral stocktaking, *cheshbon hanefesh,* occurs. Nor do we repent only our wrongdoings against God — *bein Adam lamakom;* equally important is it to obtain forgiveness for any sin against our fellow humans — *bein adam lachaveiro*. The wrongs committed against another person must be righted before pardon is requested of God.

The Talmud speaks highly of the role and benefits of repentance. "Teshuva is exceedingly great. It reaches to the throne of the Almighty; it adds years to the life of the individual; it hastens the final redemption" (Yoma 86). Both the individual and the nation gain from its effects.

Selichot

"AT MIDNIGHT," says the Psalm, "I rise to praise Thee." At midnight Jews throughout the world will attend the first Selichot (penitential) services, beginning with the words, *b'motzaei menucha*, "At the departure of the day of rest we come early before you. Turn Thine ear from on high, Thou who dwellest among the prayers of Israel, and listen to our song and prayer."

The spiritual influence and refreshment of Shabbat encourage fuller concentration on our religious duties, enabling us to carry them out with fervour and enthusiasm.

At least four days of Selichot must precede Rosh Hashana. If the New Year starts on a Tuesday, the penitential prayers are begun a week earlier. (The Sephardim recite them throughout Ellul.)

This law is derived from the Temple sacrifices, which had to be set aside for four days to make certain that they were free from permanent blemish. Similarly, the Jew must have at least four days in which to examine himself and to remove his spiritual blemishes before standing before his Maker on the Day of Judgement.

Not so long ago it was customary on the Continent for the synagogue beadle, or the *schulklopfer,* to knock three times on the door or window shutter of every Jewish home, calling out, "Israel, O holy people, awake, rise for Selichot. Arouse yourself to worship the Creator."

The prayers originated during talmudic times and are based on biblical poetry, describing the sufferings of the Jewish people in the lands of their dispersion. They have been added to throughout the ages and their main theme is centred on God's thirteen attributes of mercy, the *shelosh esreh middot* (Exodus 34: 6-7).

Viddui, the alphabetical arrangement of confession, is an essential part of forgiveness and is phrased in the plural — *ashamnu* (we have transgressed), *bagadnu* (we have dealt treacherously). The entire community regards itself responsible for the offences committed by the individual.

Every Jew is part of the totality of

"Israel, O holy people, awake, rise for Selichot. Arouse yourself to worship the Creator."

Israel. Every Jew must care not simply about his own actions and good name, but those of Klal Yisrael, the entire Jewish people. As the Talmud says: *Kol Yisrael areivin zeh bazeh,* all Israel are intertwined.

However occupied a person may be with his day-to-day affairs and his material benefits, during the Selichot period he has an opportunity to stand back and to hear the small still voice of conscience, reminding him of his Creator and the source of all good.

The story is told of a father and son walking through a forest. The child wanted to pick some berries, and the father, sensing his son's excitement, allowed him to tarry, despite the fact that it was getting dark.

He told the boy, however: "Hurry and gather your berries, but make sure we do not lose each other. Shout from time to time, 'Father, can you hear me?' and I shall answer, 'I hear you.' So long as we hear each other, we shall know that we have not lost one another'."

An order of Selichot was compiled in the ninth century by Amram Gaon, who wrote down the daily prayers in his now-famous Siddur. In time the Selichot literature grew, drawing in poetic compositions which described the misery, and the hopes, of a scattered people. The descriptions of heroic deeds thus helped to strengthen the solidarity of the people.

Judaism teaches that no one is so

bad that he cannot change for the better, nor anyone so good that he cannot become better still. The penitential period offers time for contemplation on such questions as, "How have I used my time?", "What can I do to improve?" Says the Talmud: "As you entered this world without sin, so may you depart from it without sin."

Nor is there any intermediary between man and God. Every person may approach the Creator on his own initiative. "Great is repentance, for it reaches the very throne of glory" (Yoma 86). One has only to admit a wrongdoing, express regret and promise to change and he will receive forgiveness.

All obstacles are removed for those who wish to repent, but the effort has to be made by the penitent. The final Amida of Yom Kippur states: "Thou givest Thy hand to sinners, and Thy right hand is extended to receive the penitent."

Books on Jewish ethical teaching, *sifrei mussar,* are an aid to self-evaluation, repentance and forgiveness. Such classical works include Mesilat Yesharim ("Path of the Upright"), by Luzzatto, Chovot Ha'levavot ("Duties of the Heart"), by Bachya ibn Pakuda, and Orchot Tzadikim ("The Ways of the Righteous"). All are available in English.

"Kashering"

THE TORAH forbids the drinking of the blood of animals and birds (though not of fish): "You shall not consume any blood either of fowl or of animal" (Leviticus 7). There are repeated warnings against consuming any blood that contains the "soul of the animal."

The Jewish dietary laws strive to prevent one from acquiring animal instincts or passions by devouring certain foods. "Only be strong that you do not eat the blood, for the blood is the life, and you may not eat the life with the flesh" (Deuteronomy 7).

Today's freezer foods and pre-packed products invariably mean that, for most people, the process of "kashering" meat and poultry, by removing all traces of blood, has already been carried out. But it is still necessary to be conversant with the procedure because, who knows, pre-koshered products may not always be available — and the butcher often does not have the time to do the koshering himself.

The "kashering" process is carried out in three stages: soaking the meat or poultry, salting it, and rinsing it after salting. For this one needs medium coarse salt, a bucket (which should not be used for any other purpose), a grooved or perforated draining-board (which can be placed at an angle), and a vessel for rinsing.

Much of the blood will have been drained once the animal or fowl is slaughtered by the shochet. The purpose of "kashering," therefore, is to remove any blood which may remain on the meat. Any coagulated blood should be washed off under a tap before the soaking begins.

To render the meat suitable for salting, it is soaked in a bucket of cold water for half an hour. It is then placed on the board, allowing free drainage, so that most of the water drips off, leaving the meat moist.

The salting process follows and *all* parts, including (and especially) folds, cracks and cuts, are liberally covered with salt. The meat is left on the board (allowing the blood to flow away freely) for a full hour. This procedure is known as *melicha*.

The salt should be thoroughly rinsed away by holding the meat three times under running water, or by pouring water over it three times. Care should be taken to ensure that the blood does not come into contact with anything kosher.

Liver, which has a high blood content, is "kashered" by roasting it over an open flame or in a special container under a grill. It should first be cut across, washed and lightly sprinkled with salt, and should be washed again before being cooked.

Any meat intended for the freezer should be "kashered" before being frozen and stored, allowing the housewife to prepare it for cooking immediately after defrosting.

The mitzva of "kashering" is one of the most vital forces in the régime of the Jewish housewife. The rabbis stress that it is the sacred task of every Jewish woman to supervise all that takes place in her kitchen, particularly since the dietary laws have no apparent reason for their observance. This category of commandments is known as *chukkim*, statutes, which must be accepted as a divine fiat.

The term "kashering" is also applied to the process of cleansing non-kosher cookers or utensils for use with kosher food, or for koshering year-round utensils — crockery,

cutlery and wine-cups (made of wood or metal) — for use on Pesach.

This is done either by putting the utensils into boiling water (*hag'ala*) or by heating the vessel until it is red-hot. In case of doubt whether or how to kasher an item it is always best to consult one's rabbi, since this area is fraught with complexities.

The purpose of the laws of kashrut is to create a régime of holiness for the Jew, which is linked to his service towards God. While good health, self-control and Jewish distinctiveness are among the reasons put forward for the dietary laws, their real purpose is summed up by the observation, "For you are a holy people to the Lord your God" (Deuteronomy 14).

As the late Leon Roth put it: "The dietary laws and daily prayers, no less then the Sabbath and the Day of Atonement, foster a life of quality and purpose. They raise the trivialities of the daily round into a continuous act of worship. They are religion-breathing household laws'."

Tefilin

WE NEED constant reminders to guide us in the ways of God according to the spirit of the Torah. "Visual aids" are sometimes needed to reinforce the mitzvot, the divine commands, which have been observed from the times of our ancestors until the present day.

One of the most important of these precepts, central to Jewish life, is the commandment to wear tefilin, to which there are no fewer than four specific references in the Torah.

The tefilin are known as *p'eir*, "glory," from the verse in Ezekiel 24, "Thy glory (tefilin) bind around your head." From this the sages declared that one should take great pride in donning the tefilin; they should look fresh at all times (by being regularly blackened) and should be handled with respect and care.

Rabbi Meir Jung wrote earlier this century: "It is the greatest mistake, based on an entire misunderstanding of human nature, to assume that men are capable of living in a world of ideas only, and can dispense with symbols that should embody these ideas and give them tangibility and visible form.

"Only the mitzva is the ladder connecting heaven and earth. The tefilin, containing among others, the commandment, 'You shall love the Lord your God with all your heart, with all your soul and with all your might,' are laid on the head, the seat of thought, and on the arm, the instrument of action, opposite to the heart, the seat of feeling. Thus are we taught that all our thoughts, feelings and actions must conform to the will of God.

"This mitzva, performed every weekday, has contributed more effectively to the preservation and furtherance of the morality of our people than have all the learned books on ethics written by our religious philosophers."

It is customary to initiate a young boy into the practice of donning tefilin a few weeks before his barmitzvah. Tefilin are not worn on Sabbaths or festivals since these days are in themselves a "sign" between man and his Creator and reminders to follow the ways of God.

The tefilin are put on before commencing shacharit, the morning

prayer. The worshipper stands throughout the preparations for the ceremony and begins by wrapping his talit around himself and saying the appropriate blessing. While the tefilin are being put on, one is not permitted to speak or even to join in the congregational responses for kaddish or kedusha.

The "hand," *tefila shel yad*, is first placed on the biceps of the left arm. It is then adjusted to rest against the heart, symbolic of the verse: "And you shall place these words on your hearts" (Deuteronomy 11).

Before tightening the strap, *retzua*, the first of two blessings is recited and the strap is then wound seven times around the forearm, below the elbow. The rest of the strap is temporarily wrapped around the palm.

The *shel yad* must be covered during prayers, the sages interpreting the verse, "And it shall be a sign *to you* on your hand" (Exodus 13), to mean that

it is a personal matter between the worshipper and his Creator.

The "head," *tefila shel rosh*, is then placed firmly above the forehead and the second blessing is recited. The strap around the palm is subsequently unwrapped and wound three times around the middle finger to the accompaniment of the verse from Hosea: "I will betroth you to myself forever; I will betroth you to myself in righteousness and in justice, in kindness and in mercy; I will betroth you to myself in faithfulness; and you shall know the Lord."

The two tefilin are considered as separate mitzvot and if for some reason only one of the boxes, *batim*, can be put on, this must be done in the correct manner and with the appropriate blessing.

At the conclusion of shacharit, the tefilin are removed in reversed order.

Tzizit

"YOU SHALL look on it and remember all the commandments of the Lord, and observe them..." (Numbers 15).

The commandments dealing with the tzitzit, fringes, clearly spell out the purpose of the law — that they shall serve as a sign, a reminder. A similar analogy is the tying of a piece of string around one's finger to remind one to do something.

The tassels placed on the four corners of a garment have, besides the immediate aim of reminding one of the mitzvot, a longer-term objective as well — to elevate the wearer to be among those "holy to your God." The tzitzit brings to mind the tzitz, the golden plate worn by the High Priest on his forehead and engraved with the words meaning "Holy to the Lord."

Remembrance of all the mitzvot is emphasised in the numerical value of the word tzitzit, which, added to the number of windings and knots, totals 613, the number of positive and negative commandments in the Torah.

Our sages taught that the observance of the mitzva of tzitzit is one of three protections (the other two are tefilin and mezuza) against defection from Judaism and its laws (Menachot 43). They quote from the verse in Ecclesiastes 4: "...and a threefold cord will not quickly be torn apart."

The mitzva of tzitzit is fulfilled by wearing a "small tallit," or arba kanfot ("four corners") throughout the day and by putting on the "large tallit," which covers the whole body, during prayer.

The Torah states: "You shall make for yourself fringes on the four corners of your garment" (Deuteronomy 22). In the first instance, however, they are usually bought ready-made. But when some of the fringes or threads have become worn, making them pasul (invalidated), one can fulfil the mitzva by replacing them oneself.

It should be remembered that the threads of the tzitzit are made lishma, for the express purpose of the mitzva; a thread manufactured for general use cannot be used for tzitzit.

A complete set of tzitzit is made up of sixteen threads, four of which are longer than the others. In each of the four corners of the garment, be it the small or large tallit, there are four holes, through which four threads (three of normal length and one longer) are inserted.

The threads are drawn equally on both sides and are tied together into a double knot near the edge of the garment, making a fringe of eight threads on each of the corners.

The long thread (the petil or shamash) is then coiled around the other seven threads in the following manner: first seven coils, then a double knot, followed by eight coils and another double knot; a further eleven coils followed by a double knot; and lastly, thirteen coils completed with another double knot. The number of coils adds up to thirty-nine, corresponding to the numerical value of the words adonai echad, "The Lord is One."

Writing in his memoirs about the first Zionist Congress, the president of the World Zionist Organisation, David Wolffsohn (1856-1914), revealed: "On Herzl's request, I came to Basle in order to make all the arrangements and preparations for the Congress.

"Among the many questions that occupied me at that time was one, not a major question, but also not a minor one, which represented to me something of the entire problematic complex which we are facing: with what flag shall we decorate the Congress hall? What colours and bunting? For we possessed no flag!

"Then it flashed through my mind: but, indeed, we do have a flag! It is white and blue: the tallit and tzitzit in which we enwrap ourselves during prayers. This is our coat of arms, our

Drawing by FREDA MILLER

emblem! Let us take out the tallit and tzitzit and unfurl them before the eyes of all Israel, before the eyes of all the nations."

One may use someone else's tallit for prayer, even though he has not given his permission to do so (the borrower must, of course, return it after use). This, say the rabbis, is because no Jew should object to his property being used by someone else for the purpose of fulfilling a mitzva, so long as it is not damaged in any way.

The tallit and arba kanfot, sanctified by the Torah, may not be thrown away once they have become worn. They should be buried in the same way as one buries old and torn prayer-books or pages from other holy books.

The respect Judaism demands even for inanimate objects which are used for holy purposes should teach us to be even more respectful towards human beings made in the image of God.

The two symbols of Israel

THE TWO symbols of the State of Israel, as any Jewish schoolchild will tell you, are the seven-branched menora surrounded by olive branches, and the Magen David between two blue lines.

In the choice of these motifs, considerable thought was given by the leaders of the yishuv before the final decisions were made. The menora chosen for the State emblem symbolises the candelabrum which Moses was commanded to make from a single piece of solid gold (Exodus 25:31). That same precious metal, out of which the Israelites had previously created the Golden Calf, was now to be used for a holy object, placed first in the *mishkan* (tabernacle) and later in the *bet hamikdash* (temple).

Pure gold testified to the eternal purity of the Torah and the Jewish people; the single solid block of metal symbolised the unity of *Am Yisrael*, the People of Israel. And the seven branches, wrote the eminent philosopher, Rabbi Samson Raphael Hirsch, represented not a narrow, one-sided point of view, but a diversity of ideas which, together, comprised a harmonious consensus of opinion.

Curving to seven parallel points at the apex of the central shaft, they signified equality, unity and universal enlightenment.

The menora also symbolised the creation of the universe in six days, with the centre representing the Sabbath day. Illuminating the lives of both the Jewish people and the nations of the world, it was fashioned from pure gold to encourage the Bnei Yisrael to attain high standards of ethical and moral behaviour, which would not be tarnished by the passage of time.

The menora, the work of the master craftsman, Bezalel, was designed to cast a bright and beautiful

light, for which only the purest olive oil was to be used. As the Talmud says (Menachot 53): "The olive yields its oil only by being pressed, and Israel produces what is best only when afflicted." In other words, during periods of oppression, the best qualities of our people emerge; the Jew rises to the occasion as oil rises above other liquids.

Israel's national flag was adopted well before the establishment of the State — by the Zionist Congress of 1898. The colours, blue and white, were those of the talit (prayer shawl) as specified in Numbers 15.

The design of the flag included the

Magen David as a central motif. The ornamental star, formed of two superimposed triangles, had, like the menora, been a symbol of Judaism for many centuries.

Of it, the Jewish philosopher, Franz Rosenzweig (1886-1929), wrote in "Star of Redemption": "Having fashioned the world, God chose man for a special task. The world is man's laboratory. Man must strive eternally — in life he finds God. Judaism holds the completed star — it is Israel's symbol. Through inward growth, Israel can fashion the star for all humanity."

The blue stripes above and below the Magen David are taken from the design of the talit, reminding one of Jewish tradition, custom and worship. They symbolise the eternal aspirations of a people whose roots are embedded in the Bible and whose values are designed to guide humanity.

These values, the very *raison d'être* of the Jewish State, are designed to bring spiritual light to Jewry and to mankind as a whole; to spread education, science and culture; and to highlight the true meaning of life as prescribed by the Torah.

The blue and white adopted for both the emblem and the flag are those of the original talit. White represents peace, purity and innocence; sky-blue signifies the colour of the horizon and indicates the limits of human perception in the ways of God.

"It is the colour," wrote Hirsch, "which, at the limit of our horizon, seems to point to a realm beyond human sight, representing the godliness which is revealed to us, the colour of God's bond with man, the sign of spirituality, of godliness, permeating and directing the whole life of a pure human being."

Glossary

A

Afikoman – Last item (of Matza) eaten on Seder night
Ahavat Haberiyot – Love of mankind
Ahavat Hashem – Love of God
Aleinu – Concluding prayer at end of every service
Aleph Bet – Hebrew Alphabet
Aliya – 'Ascent' to the Reading of The Law. Term also denotes immigration to Israel.
Aliya La 'Torah – 'Called-up' to Reading of the Law
Almemar – The elevated platform in Synagogue, Reader's desk
Am Ha'aretz — An ignoramus
Amida – The standing prayer
Am Kadosh – A holy people
Ammud – Reading-stand
Am Yisrael – 'The People of Israel'
Aninut – Period between death and burial
Anshei Knesset–Hagedola – Men of the Great Assembly
Aravot—Willows
Arba'a Minim – The four species (citron, palm branch, myrtles, willows)
Arba Kanfot—lit. 'four corners', under garment worn by males
Aron Hakodesh – Holy Ark
Asara Batlanim – Ten idlers
Asarah B'Tevet – The tenth of Tevet
Aseret Yemei Teshuva – The Ten Days of Penitence
Atzai Chayim – The two handles of the Torah Scroll
Aufruff – 'Calling up' to the Torah of a groom before his marriage
Aveilut – Mourning
Avoda – Service of High Priest in Holy of Holies

B

Ba'Al Koreh/Keriah – Title for person who reads the Law
Ba'Al Tekiah – Person who blows shofar
Ba'Al Teshuva – Penitent
Bakasha – Petition
Bar–Mitzvah – 'Son of the commandment'
Bat–Mitzvah – 'Daughter of the Commandment'
Batim – 'Boxes' used for phylacteries
B'Chor – First-born (boy)
Bechira —The free will
Bedikat Chametz – Search for leaven
Bein Adam Lachaveiro – Between man and his neighbour
Bein Adam Lamakom – Between man and God
Bein Hametzarim – The 'three weeks' culminating with Tisha B'Av
Beracha – Blessing
Bet Haknesset – Synagogue
Bet Hamidrash – House of learning
Bet Hamikdash – Temple
Bet Hatefila – House of prayer
Beth Din – House of judgement
Bikkur Cholim – Visiting the sick

Bima – The elevated platform in Synagogue
Birkat Hagomel – A prayer of gratitude
Birkat Hamazon – Grace after meals
Birkat Hashachar – Morning blessings
Biur Chametz – Burning of leaven
Brit Mila – Circumcision
Busha – Shame

C

Chag Ha'Asif – Festival of the ingathering (Tabernacles)
Chag Ha'Aviv – Festival of Spring
Chag Habikkurim – Festival of the First Fruits
Chag Hakatzir – The Feast of the Harvest
Chag Hamatzot – Festival of Unleavened Bread (another name for Passover)
Chag Hashavuot – The Festival of Weeks
Chag Ha'Succot – The Festival of Tabernacles
Chaim – Life
Challot –White loaves
Chametz– Leaven
Chanfan – Flatterer
Chanucah – Festival of Dedication (lights)
Chanufa – Flattery
Chanukat Habayit – Dedication of the house
Chatan Bereshit – 'Bridegroom of Genesis'
Chatan Torah – 'Bridegroom of the Law'
Chavivim Yesurim – Suffering is precious
Chazan – Reader for Services. Cantor
Chazanut – Cantorial art
Cheshbon Hanefesh – Spiritual and moral stocktaking
Chinuch – Education
Chol Hamoed – The intermediate days of Festivals
Choshen – Breastplate
Chozer Bitshuva – Penitant
Chukat Hagoy – Gentile practices
Chukim – Statutes
Chupa– Canopy
Churban – The national destruction
Chutzpa – Arrogance
Cohen – Priest

D

Dalut – Poverty
Dan L'Chaf Zechut – To judge meritoriously
Dayan– Judge
Derech Eretz – Respect; correct behaviour
D'veikut – Attachment to God

E

Eicha – Book of Lamentations
Eid Sheker – Lying witness
Em – Mother
Emet – Truth
Emuna – Faith
Eretz Yisrael – Land of Israel
Etrog – Citrus
Ezrat Nashim – Ladies gallery or section

F

G

Gabbai – Warden of congregation or Treasurer
Gam Zu L'Tova – 'This also is for good'
Ganav – Thief
Gazlan – Burglar
Gelila – Rolling together of the Torah after having been read
Gemara – Talmud
Gematria – Numerical value
Gemilut Chasadim – Kindly acts
Genevat Da'At – Stealing the mind
Get – Bill of divorce
Gittin – Bills of divorce

H

Hachnasat Orchim – Hospitality
Hadassim – Myrtles
Haftara – Passage from Book of Prophets
Hagada – 'To relate' – book used for Seder Service
Hagba'ha – Lifting up of the Torah after having been read
Hakafot – Ceremonial circuits
Hakarat Hachet – Acknowledgment of transgression
Hakarat Tova – Gratitude
Halachot – Religious laws
Halbanat Panim – To shame a person in public
Ha'Motzi – Blessing over bread
Hasagat Gevul – Encroachment
Hashkafa – Outlook
Hatarat Nedarim – Absolution of vows
Hatikva – National anthem of the State of Israel
Havdalah – Ceremony at conclusion of Sabbath or Festival
Heichal – Sanctuary
Hidur – Zeal and embellishment in religious observance

I

Ikkar – Principal or core
Ir Miklat – City of refuge

J

K

Kabala L'Haba – Resolution for future sinless behaviour
Kabbalat Shabbat – Inauguration of the Sabbath
Kaddish – A prayer which sanctifies and glories God's name
'Kashering' – The process of removing blood from meat and poultry
Kashrut – Dietary laws
Kavana – Meditation, Concentration
Kedushat Halashon – Sanctity of speech
Kehila – Community
Kehila Kedosha – Holy congregation

Keter Torah – Shape of crown placed on Torah Scroll
Ketuba – Marriage document
Kiddush – Sanctification prayer over wine
Kiddush Halevana – Sanctification of the new moon
Kiddush Hashem – Sanctification of God's name
Kiddushin – Sanctification (at marriage service)
Kinat Sofrim – A modern idiom for 'academic rivalry'
Kissei Shel Eliyahu – 'Chair of Elijah', used at circumcision
K'Lal Yisrael – The totality of Jewry
Klei Kodesh – Rdigious appurtenances
Knesset Yisrael – The brotherhood of Israel
Kol D'Avid Rochamona L'Tav Avid – 'Everything the Merciful One does, He does for good'
Kol Hane'Arim – Ceremony for 'all the youngsters' on Simchat Torah
Kol Yisrael Areivin Zeh Bazeh – 'All Israel are intertwined'
Kotel Ma'aravi – The Western Wall
Kriat Hatorah – Reading of the Law
K'Tav Ashuri – Ashkenazi type of script
Kvittel – A written plea

L

Lag B'Omer – 33rd Day of Omer period
Lashan Hara – Slander
Lashon Nekiya – Clean and refined speech
Lishma – For the sacred purpose for which the item is to be used
L'Shon Hakodesh – 'The holy tongue', Hebrew
Lulav – Palm branch

M

Ma'ariv – Evening service
Machaloket – Argument
Machaloket Leshem Shamayim – Differences for the sake of heaven
Machzor – 'Cycle'. Festival prayer book
Maftir – Repetition of last few verses of the Sidra. Person given this honour
Magen David – 'Star or Shield of David'. Six-pointed star
Ma Nishtana – Opening two words of childrens' song during the Seder
Maot Chittin – Money for matza wheat (charity)
Matza – Unleavened bread
Mayim Chaim – A 'fountain of living water'
Mechitza – 'Separation' between men's and women's sections in Synagogue
Megila – Scroll.
Megilat Esther – Scroll of Esther
Menorah – Lamp, used in Temple, also during Chanucah
Met– Death
Mezuman – Term for three to recite grace
Mezuza – 'Doorpost' case
Mikdash M'at – Miniature sanctuary
Mikva – Ritual pool of water

Mincha – Afternoon service
Minhag – Custom
Minyan – Congregational quorum of ten males
Mishkan – Tabernacle
Mishloach Manot – Sending of gifts (on Purim)
Mitzva – Commandment
Mizrach – 'East'
Moed – Festival
Musaf – Additional service

N

Na'Anuim – Waving of the 'four species'
Neginot – Musical notation for reading of the Scrolls
Neila – 'Concluding' service of Yom Kippur
Ner Tamid – Perpetual Light
Netiah Shel Simcha – Joyous planting
Netilat Yadayim – Washing of the hands
Nichum Aveilim – Comforting the mourners
Nusach – Mode of service or prayer

O

Or – Light

P

Parnas – Warden of congregation
Parochet – Curtain in front of Ark
Parshiyot – Sections of the weekly portion of the Law
Pasul – Unfit for the purpose of fulfilling the commandment
Pesach – Passover
Pesukei D'zimra – 'Passages of Song' recited at beginning of morning service
Pidyon Haben – Redemption of the first-born
Pikuach Nefesh – Danger to life
Piyyutim – Liturgical hymns, poems
Purim – Feast of Lots

R

Ra'ashon – 'Greger', rattle
Rabbi – Spiritual leader of community
Rechilut – Gossip
Rimmonim – Two finials or bells on the Torah Schroll
Rosh Chodesh – New Moon (month)
Rosh Hashana – New Year
Ruach – Atmosphere

S

Sandek – Godfather
Seder – 'Order'
Seder Tefilot – Order of prayers
Sefirat Ha'Omer – Counting of the Omer
Selichot – Penitential prayers
Seuda – Special festive meal
Seuda Hamafseket – Last meal before a fast
Seudat Havra'a – First meal eaten by mourners

Seudat Mitzva – Festive meal
Shabbat – Sabbath
Shabbat Hagadol – The 'Great Sabbath' (before Passover)
Shacharit – Morning service
Shadai – Almighty
Shalom – Peace
Shalom Bayit – Domestic Harmony
Shalosh Regalim – The three Pilgrim Festivals
Shavuot – Feast of Weeks
Shechina – Divine Presence
Shechita – Ritual slaughtering of animals and fowl
Shefichat Damim – Bloodshed
Shehecheyanu – Special blessing for new items or occasions
Sheliach Tzibur – Messenger of the congregation, Reader of Services. Chazan or Cantor
Shelosh Esreh Middot – God's thirteen attributes
Sheloshim – First thirty days of mourning
Shel Rosh – 'Of head' – (of Tefillin)
Shel Yad – 'Of hand' (of Tefillin)
Shema – 'Hear'. The first word of the Jewish declaration of faith, recited morning and night
Shemini Atzeret – Festival, 'Eighth Day of Assembly'
Shemita – Sabbatical year
Sheva Berachot – Seven blessings (at wedding)
Shinui Hashem – Change of name
Shir Shel Yom – Psalm of the day
Shiva – Seven days' mourning period
Shiva Asar B'Tammuz – The seventeenth day of Tammuz (fast day)
Shiva Denechemta – Seven weeks of comfort (between *Tisha B'Av* and *Rosh Hashana*)
Shofar – Ram's horn
Shulchan Aruch – Code of Jewish Law
Siddur – Prayer-book
Sidra – Weekly portion of the Torah
Simchat Torah – Festival, 'Rejoicing of the Law'
Siyum – Completion of a tractate (of Talmud)
Siyum Ha'Torah – Completion of the Torah Scroll
Sofer – Scribe
Sofer Ha'Kahal – Recording clerk of the Beth Din and communal public notary
Sofer S'Tam – Scribe engaged in writing the principal religious appurtenances of the community
Sofrim – Scribes
Succa – Booth
Succot - Festival of Tabernacles
S'vivon – 'Dreidle', spinning top

T

Ta'anit Chalom – A fast observed after a bad dream
Ta'anit Esther – The fast of Esther
Taggin – Crown of three prongs or strokes ornamenting certain letters in the Torah
Taharat Hamishpacha – Family purity
Takkanot – Congregations' written regulations
Tallit – Prayer shawl

Talmud – literary collection of discussions on the Torah text

Tamid – Daily offering in thc Temple

Taryag – '613' – total number of commandments in the Five Books of Moses

Tashmishei Kedusha – Religious appurtenances

Tefila – Prayer

Tefila Betzibur – Public worship

Tefilat Geshem – Prayer for rain

Tefillin – Phylacteries

Tehila – Praise

Teiva – Box or chest

Teshuva – Repentance

Tevilat Keilim – Immersion of new utensils

Tikkun Leil Shavuot – Anthology for Festival of Weeks night.

Todah – Thanks

Torah – Scroll of the Law (from 'Horah', to teach, to instruct)

Torah Sheb'alpeh – The Oral Law

Torah Shebiktav – The Written Law

Tu Bishvat – New Year for Trees

Tza'ar Gidul Banim – 'Pain of raising children'

Tzaddik – A righteous person

Tzedaka – Charity

Tzedek – Justice

Tzitz – Breastplate

Tzniut – Modesty

U

Uman – Craftsman

V

Viddui – Confession

Y

Yad – Pointer, used for reading of the Law

Yamim Noraim – The High Holy-days

Yashrut B'Masa Uve'Maton – Uprightness in business transactions

Yesurim Shel Ahava – Suffering inflicted by divine love

Yom Ha'Atzmaut – Israel Independence Day

Yom Hashoa – Holocaust Memorial Day

Yom Hazikaron – Memorial Day

Yom Kippur – Day of Atonement

Yom Yerushalayim – Jerusalem Day

Yosher – Fairness

Yovel – Jubilee year

Z

Zechut – Merit

Zechut Avot – Merit of the Fathers

Zerizut – Alertness

Zemirot – Table hymns

Z'Man Matan Torateinu – 'Season of the Giving of the Law', (Festival of Pentecost)

Z'Man Simchateinu – 'Season of our Rejoicing', (Festival of Tabernacles)

Z'Reezim U'Makdeemin – To be diligent and hasten to perform a mitzva